Archery
A MILITARY HISTORY

Fifteenth-century francs archers *from the painted hangings at Rheims*

Archery

A MILITARY HISTORY

E.G. Heath

OSPREY

First published in 1980 by
Osprey Publishing Limited,
12–14 Long Acre, London WC2E 9LP
A Member Company of the George Philip Group

British Library Cataloguing in Publication Data
Heath, Ernest Gerald
    Archery.
    1. Bow and arrow—History
    I. Title
    355.8'2   U877

ISBN 0 85045 353 4

Printed in Great Britain by
Butler & Tanner Ltd, Frome and London

Contents

A Historical Perspective

Over the centuries the arts of war have undergone radical changes due to a complexity of causes, and with those changes weapons of greater refinement and increased lethal power have replaced earlier more primitive and less effective aids to sudden death. In the ages of the world when civilizations were less complex than they are today, arms were simple and the discipline of troops imperfect, but it would appear that as man became more enlightened he invented more sophisticated forms of weaponry; combat became a science and the whole business of war rapidly reached the stage whereby battles are resolved by slide-rule and computer rather than by siege, pillage and hand-to-hand combat. It is not for us to argue the advantage of one circumstance or another, but the truth is that in battle the vanquished army is that which has the greatest losses in manpower, that which has been starved of supplies, or suffers a loss of strategic advantage, or a combination of all three. The final analysis of a conflict depends largely on the side the individual happens to support.

The simplest way to win a battle is to subjugate the foe, and this premise has been the overriding intention in warfare both ancient and modern. The path of history is strewn with the casualties of war and its course has been shaped by the conflicts in which they took part. The methods adopted to secure victory have ranged from the unpreparedness of inter-tribal conflict, where only the fittest have survived, to a systematically planned and organized campaign utilizing every skill in the art of war. It is perhaps a surprising thought that the weapon with which we are concerned, the bow and arrow, has probably been responsible for more casualties in war than any other weapon man has invented. It predates by many hundreds of years *blitzkrieg* tactics, the employment of snipers, armour-piercing missiles and even psychological warfare.

The bow is not only the earliest mechanical device used in warfare in which stored energy is utilized, but it also has the distinction of having been used in battle for a very long period of time in every part of the world as a principal weapon of offence. Our story gives emphasis to the part played by the individual who used this weapon in every sort of conflict in the primitive and civilized worlds, which, although a record of co-operative endeavour for the most part, nevertheless underlies the uniqueness of the bow in that one individual is solely responsible for its operation. The experience of shooting this weapon, even in the height of battle, is singularly a personal one. None the less the effect of an accurately shot arrow is just as lethal, and arguably more humane, than the effect of a hydrogen bomb.

It has advantages over more modern personal weapons. It is easy to train soldiers in its use, it is comparatively cheap, it is portable and silent in operation. It lends itself to a variety of uses, and there are other unique qualities which the ingenuity of military commanders could put to good use. These characteristics will be illustrated as the history of the warlike rôle of the bow unfolds.

The evolution of this weapon has been carefully traced by means of archaeological and documentary evidence, and this record of man's most persistent weapon spans some 50,000 years of his existence. Gad Rausing, whose important monograph on the origins and development of the bow has been acknowledged as the first overall survey of this subject, commenced his work with these words: 'The bow, and more particularly the composite bow, is technically one of the most complicated and most advanced artefacts among those of perishable materials.'

At a conservative guess, based on archaeological reasoning, the invention of the bow probably took place in the early part of the late Paleolithic, perhaps in the Perigordien or the Aurignacien. Subsequently its discovery seems to have occurred over and over again in widely separated parts of the world, although in some cases there is a clear line

8

of descent. The bow differs from all other early weapons in being able to store the energy supplied by human muscle. On release, this pent-up energy is suddenly transferred to the arrow, which can thus be projected at a much higher velocity than that at which it can be thrown by hand.

The conventional construction of a bow is universally familiar—a stave of some flexible material, the two ends of which are connected by a string. Similarly the missile shot from this weapon is instantly recognizable—a straight shaft with a point at one end and feathers at the other, the conventional constituent parts of the arrow. But there the simplicity of description stops, for the bow itself can be of a wide variety of forms and materials and the arrow has been made in a bewildering number of designs which have never been subjected to an overall study.

The techniques of bowyery and the uses of archery were well established in north-western Europe by late Mesolithic and Neolithic times, and the skills of archery were commonly practised by hunters, but no doubt also by warriors. Much could be added regarding the technical aspects of prehistoric archery, methods of manufacture, tools, forms of arrow-heads, and possibly shooting techniques, and a wealth of data is readily available to support such accounts. Of special value in such research is the study of existing primitive societies who have somehow managed to side-step the benefits of civilization and who have survived in a state of culture close to that of prehistoric man. Many of these tribes used the bow and arrow until comparatively recent times, and a few still regard the bow as their principal weapon for survival. From studies of such primitive peoples we can formulate a picture of the type of feuding warfare which was probably the limit of aggression among prehistoric groups where the bow was used as the main weapon.

The simple segment self-bow of northern Europe spread all over the Continent with the immigrating Germanic tribes; before long it fell out of use and survived nowhere but in England. This was the forerunner of the traditional English longbow, although, erroneously, the Welsh flat-bow has sometimes been claimed as having that distinction.

The subsequent history of the simple stick and string which became the legendary weapon of the English, and how it earned eternal fame particularly during the Hundred Years War, will be discussed more fully in due course.

9

Regretfully there are fewer relics of bows and arrows from the Middle Ages than there are from the prehistoric eras, but this is compensated for by detailed accounts written by contemporary chroniclers and historians from which has emerged a clear picture of the medieval bowman and his weapon and the conditions under which he found himself when on active service.

Whereas the longbow and other bows of self-wood construction were made exclusively of wood in one or more pieces, the composite bow had limbs constructed of layered materials so arranged that the tension and compression in the bent limbs occurred in those materials best adopted to withstand those forces. Horn, which is compressible, was used as the belly of the bow—the side nearest the archer; sinew, which has elastic properties, was used for the opposite face, the back; and the whole was built up on a wooden core of several specially shaped pieces joined together, and then covered with moisture-proof lacquers. When released the horn belly acted like a coiled spring, returning instantly to its original position. Sinew, on the other hand, contracts after being stretched, which is exactly what happens to the convex back of the bow. The combined pushing and pulling of the horn and pulling of the sinew straightens the bow when the string is released with much greater speed than could any known wood, and this ingenious arrangement enabled a shorter and faster-reacting bow to be constructed.

It is remarkable to recall that this technological advance in bow design was employed over a wide territory as distant as Mesopotamia, Siberia and Japan and even among certain tribes of north-western America. Rausing describes the idea of creating an artificial elasticity by adding one or more carefully chosen layers of materials to a bow stave to increase the power and cast of the weapon, no less than a 'technological break-through of the first order of magnitude for prehistoric man, who could only use nature for a pattern for his creative work'. It was also a phenomenon that opened up vast possibilities in the field of battle; at once there was a weapon capable of easy manœuvre, discharging a missile with extra force and therefore greater range and penetrative power.

The bow has had a highly complex descent in terms of technology. Thousands of years of bowyers in almost every part of the world have whittled away at their bow staves, adding an improvement here, rejecting a failure there, until a wide range of types was evolved each suited to the particular environment in which they were fashioned. The accumulated knowledge of these matters is very comprehensive, but as our principal intention is to describe how these weapons were used, the warriors who used them and the events with which bows and arrows became so much a part, we have only given an outline of the various bow types.

At this stage the reader, whose interest, hopefully, in this quite extraordinary weapon has been aroused, might, quite properly, say—What about the arrow, without which the bow would be useless? Did not this component, man's first mechanically propelled missile, play an equally vital part in the archery of war? And did it not have an equally interesting evolutionary pattern? Surely there must have been a range of different sorts of arrows to 'go with' the different types of bows described, certain arrows made for special purposes, designs to fulfil particular requirements, a typology from which individual forms can be recognized as typical of one sort of culture, place, or time?

Our answer to that question is that the omission is deliberate, because from time to time as our story unfolds, references will be made to those specialities of the fletcher's art which play a part in the narrative. To begin to describe the range of arrow-heads that has been provided for one culture alone would fill a couple of chapters. For example, if we take the recent studies of Brazilian Indians and assume that they are typical of a primitive bow-using culture, there have been identified no less than forty-one different forms of arrow-heads of ten different materials which they use, which may be added to five types of arrow-shafts, which can be fletched in a dozen different ways. Therefore, the possible total range which could be found amongst these peoples is a very extended order indeed. This example is of a primitive culture; the odds are that the range would be even greater—if it were ever known—among the archer-peoples of the Western World and those of Asia. Thus our reason for being selective is that not only would it be difficult to present an account of the evolution of the arrow, even briefly, it would be unnecessary for our story. The comparative lethal qualities of one arrow with another depends principally on the power and direction of its flight, which has been generated by the bow from which it has been shot. There are, to be sure, in addition considerations as to the design of the arrow itself, but without the kinetic force which drives it to its mark any arrow would be impotent.

Since man became a reasoning animal somewhere in the world there has been conflict. Jealousy between individuals became feuds, bullying between families erupted into tribal conflict, ambition between nations exploded into full-scale war, there have been battles over religion, struggles for political power or succession, money, prestige, and a hundred and one other causes have produced an endless roll of belligerent engagements. Whether or not these acts of aggression are honourable or dishonourable depends entirely on which side you happen to be, or according to the interpretation of the event by historians.

The past can only be recalled by factual evidence and a strong imagination. The interpretation of the former depends largely on the quality of the latter. In this book we have leaned heavily on the primary sources of history, the chroniclers and the first-hand accounts of events, but we have also drawn on the fund of knowledge prepared by specialists in the study of warfare.

The rôle of the bow in history, and in particular the part it has played in bloody conflict, is considerable and extends across many thousands of years of the history of man. During that period of time this weapon has been rejected by one nation and adopted by another, it has been revered as a war weapon *par excellence* by some and regarded with contempt by others. These changes can be related to many factors concerned with the rise and fall of civilizations, social and economic change, and the constant movement of peoples over the face of this earth. Our opening theme suggested such a pattern of change in warfare, and the varied rôles of the bow and the way in which it was regarded are only secondary to the men who used it to defend their liberties or to pursue aggression.

Our story of the bow in war does not deal with inanimate museum objects, browsing over campaign maps, gazing at dioramas reconstructing brief moments of time, or the academic study of strategy and tactics; it deals rather with the horsemen of the Steppes, the Yeomen of England, the Indians of the Plains and the armies of the Orient, all capable of bringing to life the bows that they used and that they knew so well.

CHAPTER 1

Bows of War

A Sumerian bowman in action, using a composite segment bow. A fragment of a bas-relief from about the end of the fourth millennium

At a time when the Neolithic population of Great Britain was being driven north and west by the megalith builders migrating from the Mediterranean, a great civilization was flourishing in Mesopotamia. The Sumerians, a non-Semitic people, who lived from 3500 BC onwards in the fertile riverine region between modern Baghdad and the Persian Gulf, and between the Tigris and the Euphrates, are renowned as the inventors of cuneiform writing, which was adopted by all the peoples of the Near East. The historical record of this multiplicity of city states, more often than not at war with each other, has been preserved in this unique form of script, and describes guerilla warfare with invaders from the east and battles with conquerors from the north.

Throughout Mesopotamia at this time certain principles of warfare and basic types of weapons and fortifications were established, which set the pattern for the succeeding 3,000 years. The means of mobility, methods of attack, security, protection and defence, all have their origin at this time, and the Sumerians developed a system of warfare that was remarkable for its methodical and disciplined organization. A disorganized rabble in battle without cohesion or proper command is useless, and the Sumerian commanders quickly learnt the subtle advantage of having forces at their command which were malleable and controllable. This era saw the beginnings of such principles, and such matters gradually became fully established as methods of warfare which were faithfully repeated whenever battles took place over the next several thousand years until the use of gunpowder in the fourteenth century AD.

13

In the relatively small area of fertile land that became Sumeria and Babylonia, warfare was inevitably more or less a continuous process because the inhabitants of the valleys fought each other for possession of the precious well-watered land, and they also had to defend themselves against the jealous peoples of the desert. But occasionally these raids developed into much bigger onslaughts when great masses of migratory peoples, Semitic and then Indo-European, were attracted to the river valleys. The first great clash of cultures in history, between the Sumerians and the Semites for dominance over Mesopotamia, began a series of struggles which continued for thousands of years.

The first half of the third millennium in Mesopotamia saw the introduction of the battle chariot, and the military impact of this innovation was revolutionary. It was in general use as a basic instrument of war throughout Mesopotamia at this time, and surprisingly it was not until some 1,200 years after that it was first used in Egypt. The chariots were used mainly for direct assault on the enemy and not for flanking movements at medium range. At first the fighting men in these chariots were armed with the javelin and spear, but the later improvement of a light, spoked wheel, a lightweight body and faster horses increased mobility and manœuvrability, and turned the chariot into an effective mobile firing platform. Although the bow, the only effective long-range weapon, had been in fairly general use certainly since the end of the fourth millennium, it was not used by charioteers until after 2000 BC, by which time the heavy and clumsy Mesopotamian battle vehicle had undergone the improvements we have mentioned.

The power of Sumer was finally merged with that of the Semitic Akkadians of Babylonia, who added the decisive factor of archery to the Sumerian order of battle. The soldier-king Naram-Sin and his generals utilized the full potential of the composite bow as a warlike weapon, conquering Mesopotamia and the Sumerians and even reaching the Mediterranean. The principle of co-operation between infantry and artillery, together with the mobile striking force of the chariot, became standard military practice, and monuments commemorating long-forgotten battles show the phalanx of infantry armed with spears and swords, charioteers, and long-range archers operating together in full co-ordination. One of the most important of these

14

This relief, from the late Hittite palace of Sam'al, vividly shows the effectiveness of the use of archery from chariots, which by that time had become lighter and faster and were in fairly general use in the Middle East

This relief, from the late Hittite palace of Sam'al, vividly shows the effectiveness of the use of archery from chariots, which by that time had become lighter and faster and were in fairly general use in the Middle East

monuments is the victory stele of Naram-Sin, found at Susa, which shows the triumphant monarch in full regalia treading his enemies underfoot and carrying in his left hand, as a symbol of power, the composite bow and in his right an arrow. The type of bow carried by Naram-Sin is unmistakably a composite of a double concave form which fell out of use after the fall of the Sumerian Empire.

One of the most important battles in early history was between the Egyptians and the Hittites. A late Hittite kingdom endured with varying fortune from *c.* 1200 to 709 BC and from it mercenaries were provided for the Hebrew army and even ladies for Solomon's harem. Friction with the Egyptians was generated by the Hittites gaining control of Syria in 1340 BC, and the pharaoh Seti I campaigned to recover the Egyptian grip. Finally, in 1286 BC, Rameses II fought a great battle at Kadesh against the Hittites, in which the Hittites gained the advantage.

The Battle of Kadesh on the Orontes is so well described in Egyptian written accounts and so widely illustrated in reliefs, that it is possible to reconstruct it in all its minutiae. In these accounts the course of the battle can be traced with all the classic ingredients of warfare; preparations for a siege, surprise attack, counter-attack, manœuvre and out-manœuvre, even accounts of spies and looting are included.

The Egyptian force included mercenaries from Canaan, a crack unit of specially picked young men, probably a com-

A group of Nubian mercenary archers serving in the Egyptian armies of the South, carrying self-wood, recurved bows. A wooden model from the tomb of Masahti (c. 2100–1788 BC)

The victorious Naram-Sin triumphantly treading his enemies underfoot and armed with a very early representation of a composite bow (c. 2500 BC)

pany of Nubian bowmen using simple double convex bows, and the mobile archers armed with long-range composite bows in fast, light chariots. Throughout the written history of this period there are vivid accounts of the chariot in battle which must have struck fear into the enemy. The prophet Nahum, writing of such an incident, said: 'The noise of a whip, and the noise of the rattling of the wheels, and of the prancing horses, and of the jumping chariots. The horsemen lifteth up both the bright sword and the glittering spear: and there is a multitude of slain and a great number of carcases.'

The chariots were fitted with quivers for supplies of arrows and a case was provided to prevent the bow warping when not in use. The arrows had shafts of reed and arrowheads of bronze which had superseded those of flint of earlier times. The foot-archer carried on a shoulder-strap a quiver of up to about thirty arrows. Archery training in

17

the Egyptian army was a popular pastime and practice ranges were available under the supervision of experienced instructors. Part of this training stressed the importance of shooting from a chariot with the horses in full gallop—no mean accomplishment, particularly in battle conditions. Up to about 1500 BC Egyptian soldiers wore no armour, but from that time charioteers and bowmen, who had to have both hands free and therefore could not carry shields, took to wearing helmets and a form of flexible and light mail coat made of rectangular metal scales.

Soldiers were trained from boyhood, 'being imprisoned in the barracks' and 'pummelled with beatings'. Later, they could live with their families between campaigns. Youths of the upper classes usually enlisted in the separately organized chariot corps, some of them buying their own chariots and driving home to show off their skill before battle. Between battles a soldier ate well enough, but in time of action 'his food is the grass of the field like any other head of cattle'. His was a hard life, according to one ancient

Detail from a relief on the temple of Rameses III at Medinet Habu. The chariot wheels are now positioned further back to provide more stability for the bowmen in action

Egyptian archers practising. The regularity with which the arrows are stacked suggests a military exercise. From a wall painting in Beni-Hasan

An arrow finds its way through a chink of scale armour. A detail from a scene painted on a chariot found in the tomb of King Thutmose IV, XVIII Dynasty (1411–1397 BC)

scribe: 'Come I will speak to you of the ills of the infantryman. He is awakened while there is still an hour for sleeping, he is driven like a jackass and he works until the sun sets beneath its darkness of night. He hungers and his belly aches. He is dead while he lives. But frightened, and calling to his god, "Come to me that you may rescue me" he fought. He fought with maces, daggers and spears on field filled with charging chariots and bronze-tipped arrows.'

Arrows shot by trained bowmen could penetrate light armour, and as the penetrating power of weapons developed, armour was correspondingly strengthened. All armour has its weak spots and a detail of a relief from the chariot of Thutmose IV shows how an arrow could pierce the weak point of the mail coat of an Asiatic charioteer at

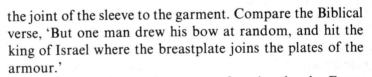

An Egyptian bow and arrow factory of the fifteenth century BC. Several processes in the manufacture of bows and arrows can be identified from this wall painting from the tomb of Menkheperra, Thebes

the joint of the sleeve to the garment. Compare the Biblical verse, 'But one man drew his bow at random, and hit the king of Israel where the breastplate joins the plates of the armour.'

The Sea Peoples, as they were referred to by the Egyptians, consisted of a number of different tribes who combined and made incursions into the lands of the eastern Mediterranean. This military rising eventually threatened Egypt and in due course it was defeated by the stronger nation. One group of the Sea Peoples, the Sherdens, served as mercenaries in the Egyptian army and also formed part of pharaoh's bodyguard. The Sea Peoples were defeated in two battles, one on land and the other at sea. The naval battle of 340 BC is most interesting in that it demonstrates how the basic difference in the weapons used affected the course of the battle. In particular we can recognize the advantage which the bow gave to the victorious Egyptians. Breasted, the Egyptologist, when describing a magnificent relief at Medinet Habu which depicts this sea battle, said

that it was 'the first naval battle on salt water of which we know anything'. The Egyptian ships are shown crowded with bowmen armed with composite bows, and the action is supported by volleys of arrows from groups of a number of four-man units of archers on shore. The exact course of the battle is not known, but the final outcome is clear and there can be no doubt that it was determined by the superiority of the Egyptian armament, which had power, long range and the capacity to pierce armour. The Egyptian four-man units of archers were also used to give covering fire to assault groups who were employed in the siege of towns and strongholds.

A four-man squad of Egyptian archers shooting from a river bank. They are clearly well disciplined and were probably used for special operations against water-borne enemies

The Assyrians were the first to use cavalry, of which they employed two specific types, bowmen and spearmen, both of which were used in short- and long-range combat. Mounted archers attacked mostly from the rear or the flanks, operating in pairs, one horseman with a bow and the other holding both sets of reins and a large shield big enough to protect two men. The horses were sometimes protected with leather armour. In the time of Ashurbanipal, chariot crews were increased from two to four; driver, archer and two shield-bearers.

The main power of the Assyrian infantry rested with its archers, who, with their highly advanced composite bows, were used in all types of attack. The Assyrian warriors were good fighters in all kinds of country, from the mountains to the marshes and the desert. In 400 years of almost incessant warfare in two empires, the Assyrians were rarely beaten, despite the fact that their armies were often outnumbered and many of their enemies were certainly as well armed as they were. Their success was due to two principal factors—most of the kings of Assyria were first-rate field commanders, and the nation was put on a proper war footing. This meant that all the resources of the state were directed to military ends, there was a regular army with compulsory military service and conquered peoples had to provide contingents for the army. The troops were well provided for by the government and at the end of a campaign a share of the spoils was divided among them. Finally, the army was backed by an efficient intelligence system, a model for armies of later centuries.

The development of siege warfare was, to a large extent, an Assyrian achievement. This was made necessary to combat the increasing resistance from smaller nations, such as Syria and Palestine, who developed the technique of fortification. The success of the Assyrian attacks was due to maximum co-ordination and exploitation of all military possibilities. For example, they used various techniques of siege—storming of ramparts, breaching of walls and gates, scaling, tunnelling and even psychological warfare. Mobile siege towers were brought into action manned by archers who gave continuous covering fire for their own troops, such as the operators of battering rams who were in great danger from defending archers and spearmen. Some sieges were heroically sustained against the Assyrians, but by far the greater number succumbed to their military superiority.

The Assyrian infantry was divided into three broad units according to weapons; spearmen, archers and slingmen. In addition all were armed with the long straight sword for hand-to-hand combat. The main power of the Assyrian infantry rested with the archers. To begin with they wore long coats of mail, even though their weight hampered movement, and, particularly in short-range action, they were sometimes accompanied by a special shield-bearer with a small round shield to protect their face. After about 750

Part of an Assyrian chariot charge led by Ashurnasirpal against enemy infantry and chariots. Each chariot had a driver and an archer, and two quivers provided an ample supply of arrows. From the palace of Ashurnasirpal II, Nimrud

BC a radical change was introduced, which included the employment of a huge shield, tall and heavy, equipped with a sort of hood or canopy and carried by a shield-bearer to protect the archer. This enabled the coat of mail to be shortened so that it covered only the top part of the body, or to dispense with it altogether. In general archers wore helmets of either a pointed shape, somewhat like an inverted funnel, or a more simple round shape. The principle of co-operation between mounted archers, spearmen and infantry became a feature of Assyrian tactics. In addition to these élite archers, who might be called the heavy archery units, the Assyrians used archers from the armies they conquered. These auxiliary units were very lightly equipped and the Assyrians did not worry unduly about their protection.

During the invasions and occupations of Egypt by the Assyrians their weapons must necessarily have been numerous in the land, and it would be remarkable if some had not been preserved. Such bows may have been valued trophies, or have been acquired in a variety of ways, but in any case their complex and beautiful structure must have favourably impressed bow-using peoples like the Egyptians.

An Assyrian siege of a walled town in which the use of the small round shield can be seen. It is also interesting to note the typical Assyrian triangular bow, both at full draw and at rest

22

The heavier and more protective full-length shield is shown here, with shield-bearer, giving special protection to an Assyrian bowman. From the reliefs at the palace of Sargon, Khorsbad (721–705 BC)

Among tomb finds which have included ancient bows were those of Rameses II, *c.* 1300 BC, whose bow was first recognized as an important relic of the history of archery in 1893. Up to then it had been incorrectly classified as a musical instrument! The weapon, of typical angular form, was possibly of Hittite or Assyrian origin, and it may have been introduced into Egypt as spoils of war or carried by foreign mercenaries. It may also have been a relic from an Egyptian invasion of Syria by Rameses when he captured Kadesh.

The decline of Assyria was watched from a distance by the Jews with very natural feelings of gratified revenge, intermingled with the nobler emotions of exultation, at the approaching overthrow of a savagely militaristic nation. They had many good reasons; for example the conquest of the kingdom of Sumeria by the Assyrians in 722 BC saw the end of northern culture and literature. Whilst probably not all the inhabitants were carried into captivity the expulsion was ruthless enough to break up the lost 'ten tribes' so completely that they vanished from history, never to reappear save in such fanciful accounts as that in the Book of Mormon. At the end of the seventh century BC the Medes, the Scythians and the Babylonians united and

23

rapidly overwhelmed Assyria, culminating in the fall of Nineveh in 612 BC. This event was achieved by a coalition of powers who had been trained in warfare by the Assyrians themselves. So complete was the defeat and enslavement, and so extensive the slaughter and deportation of the victims—a grim reminder of their own tactics—that the separate Assyrian nation ceased to exist and was more completely ruined than any other empire in history.

Cyrus II was to conquer the land of the Medes and become founder of the old Persian Empire, the great empire of the ancient world, which only flourished for some 300 years from 600 BC to about 300 BC. During the course of these three centuries, however, there unfolded on the Iranian plateau, and in the whole of the Near East, a drama so fascinating, a spectacle so fabulous and incredible, that we cannot fail to be dazzled by the insane genius, the atrocious deeds, the extravagance, and also by the greatness of some of the Median and Persian kings.

Cyrus subjugated Babylonia, putting an end to the Sem-

The Assyrian mounted archer perfected special skills in shooting from horseback. In this bas-relief from Susa the horse is standing motionless while its rider takes aim

24

itic domination of western Asia which had lasted for 1,000
years. In the east, Cyrus protected his empire against the
audacious raids of the Saka tribes of the Turanian Steppes.
In a comparatively short time after the conquests of Cyrus,
the triangular bow, common to Mesopotamia, was superseded by the recurved type, which approximated to the form
of the later Persian and Turkish bows, a pattern which
remained virtually unchanged until the eighteenth century
AD. Cyrus died in combat; he threw himself into the fray
against an invasion by Asiatic bowmen, the Massagetic
horsemen of the north, who had stormed out of the steppes
of Turkestan, incited by the Scythians. In the course of his
heroic struggle against this menace to Persia, in the summer
of 530 BC, Cyrus the Great fell victim to the wily tactics
and dangerous bowmanship of his adversaries.

In this event one may detect a deliberate attempt to pick
off the supremo by the skill of one or more bowmen detailed
for the task. There would certainly be an advantage in
breaking the morale and subduing the offensive spirit of the
adversary forces by such action. One of the recognized
objectives in the assault battles in open terrain was to try
and kill the enemy king, as in the case of the king of Israel
who suffered the fatal arrow of the archer who 'drew a bow
at random', and Josiah the king of Judah, who was mortally
wounded by an Egyptian archer at the Battle of Megiddo.
Little wonder that the bow came to be regarded as a superior
and versatile weapon.

The cavalcade of kings who occupied the throne of Persia
continued with Cambyses, who conquered Egypt and had
himself crowned pharaoh; Darius, who reconstructed the
huge Persian Empire and, after putting down dangerous
rebellions, instituted far-reaching reforms including a rigid
bureaucracy, a common currency and a standing army; and
Xerxes, who inherited Persia and allowed it to decay in a
welter of excess and extravagance. The regular army instituted by Darius was kept more or less constantly on
active service during his reign. In his palace was one wall
decorated with a magnificent frieze of polychrome tile-work
consisting of rows of archers of the royal guard, who are
known from the descriptions of the Persian Wars by Herodotus. The relief is dated about 500 BC and clearly shows
the archers, in gaily coloured uniforms, carrying their bows
with pronounced recurved ends secure in bow-cases slung

*Figure of an archer
from a frieze of such
figures representing
the Royal Guard ('The
Ten Thousand') of the
Persian kings. From
the palace of Darius,
Susa (c.500 BC)*

on each left shoulder. Darius led his armies across the Bosphorus, through Thrace and as far as the Danube. He crossed the river with a force of between 70,000 and 80,000 men and marched off into the uncharted wilderness, under constant attack by Scythian horsemen. Darius was never able to inflict a decisive defeat on the Scythians despite the magnitude of his operations, but he was one of the greatest rulers in world history, an organizer of the first order and a better practical economist than any other king before him.

In an interesting artistic convention, this composite pose of a Greek archer in action shows the bow being drawn while at the same time a fresh arrow is brought up for the next shot

To properly view the Persian Wars, which took place between 499 and 449 BC, and which can be summarized as attempts by the Persians to conquer Greece, it is helpful to look briefly at the growth of Greek warfare. The special problems that faced the Persians in battle situations involved methods of warfare new to them, and in this respect they had developed differently from the Greeks. From about 1400 BC the 'heroic' age of Greek warfare began. Battles were trials of valour between mighty warriors who would ride on to the field in chariots, dismount, and engage in single combat. The method of confronting the enemy by a solid wall of armoured troops further protected by closely overlapping shields and bristling with long thrusting spears was an effective counter to an attack by cavalry and archers, as the Persians were to discover.

There were, of course, weaknesses in the use of phalanxes of heavy infantry; the type of ground on which battles could

27

be fought was limited to level open terrain, broken continuity of the close-order line spelled disaster, and since the whole success of these tactics depended on the initial charge, the whole weight of the force was employed, leaving no reserves. Thus, in battle against the Persians, Greek victories were based on an initial defensive, fought on ground of their own choosing where the Persian cavalry would be unable to develop its full potential.

In the Persian Wars the trouble began when the Greek cities of Ionia, the coastal areas of Asia Minor, were in revolt, and the Persians, having crushed them, determined to punish the European Greeks for supporting their kinsmen. The first invasion in 490 BC, under Darius, was defeated at Marathon and driven back. The absence of archery and cavalry among the enemy forces at this battle was particularly noted by Herodotus in his contemporary military chronicle of the armies and battles of the Persians and the Greeks. The two armies had met on the plain of Marathon, 'the battle was set in array', and the Athenians opened with a spirited charge against the Persians at a distance of about 1,600 yards, with their serried ranks of hoplites bristling with spears presented forwards. 'The Persians,' reported Herodotus, 'when they saw the Greeks coming on at speed made ready to receive them, although it seemed to them that the Athenians were bereft of their senses, and bent upon their own destruction; for they saw a mere handful of men coming on at a run without either horsemen or archers.'

The surprise of the Persians at not seeing the familiar ranks of archers reflects their confidence in their own methods of warfare, which had been developed on the basis of co-operation between various arms, and their overconfidence in their own, well-tried, formula for battle; this contempt for any lesser form of warfare probably contributed to their own defeat. Robert Graves sums up a supposed 'Persian Version' of this battle in his poem of that name, which is reminiscent of national attitudes to defeat neatly turned into victory.

> Truth-loving Persians do not dwell upon
> The trivial skirmish fought near Marathon.
> As for the Greek theatrical tradition
> Which represents that summer's expedition
> Not as a mere reconnaissance in force

Amazon warriors in a fight between Greeks and Amazons. Part of the detail of the archer who is drawing her bow is missing. From the frieze of the Mausoleum from Halicarnassus (c.355–350 BC)

By three brigades of foot and one of horse
(Their left flank covered by some obsolete
Light craft detached from the main Persian fleet)
But as a grandiose, ill-starred attempt
To conquer Greece—they treat it with contempt;
And only incidentally refute
Major Greek claims, by stressing what repute
The Persian monarch and the Persian nation
Won by this salutary demonstration:
Despite a strong defence and adverse weather
All arms combined magnificently together.

Ten years later a large expedition under Xerxes crossed the Hellespont (Dardanelles) and marched into Greece, with a fleet on its left flank. At the pass of Thermopylae the Persian infantry refused to close with the hoplites and the Greeks were eventually worn down by insistent archery volleys from front and rear. The heroic force of 300 Spartans perished, and the invaders eventually occupied Athens.

In the next thirty years desultory fighting eventually restored nearly all that the Greeks had lost in Ionia and, as a significant comment on the differences between the Greek and the Persian methods of warfare, Aeschylos states that 'to the entire peoples of Greece, the Persian War appeared as the victory of the Hellenic lance over the Asiatic arrow'. In the following centuries this led to the Greeks, in their turn, overrunning Persia under Alexander the Great.

However, before this momentous event the Greeks rapidly learnt the advantages of long-range strategy and the disadvantages of the restrictive movement caused by heavily armoured troops, and from about 400 BC Greek arms began to be diversified. Light foot soldiers were cheap and their development was furthered by the growth of the mercenary system. Many Greeks who had fought in the Peloponnesian War had no other skill when it ended in 404 BC, so they became professional soldiers. In 401 Cyrus hired 10,000 Greeks to fight for him in revolt against his brother Artaxerxes, king of Persia. At the battle of Cunaxa, near Babylon, Cyrus deployed them so badly that he lost. The 'Ten Thousand' then spent five months retreating to the Black Sea, and Xenophon, one of their generals, wrote of how they learnt much about light-armed warfare, particularly archery, from the mountain tribes through which they fought their way. There are records of many other thousands of Greeks taking service as mercenaries abroad, many of them bringing back the techniques they learned, in particular from the Cretan archers and the Rhodian slingers.

A silver stater from Cydonia, Crete, of about 400–300 BC, showing a Cretan archer mercenary

The Greeks never became specially renowned for their archery, although there are scattered references to the use of the bow in their battles from *c.* 530 BC, most of which were provided by mercenaries, particularly Scythians and Cretans. Occasionally a small complement of archers was found aboard the famed Greek triremes, and selected groups of archers were used from time to time for special assignments and policing duties. Tantalizing glimpses of special uses of the bow occur now and again, such as the two-way messaged arrows at the siege of Potidaea, incendiary arrows at Plataea and the use of the bow for assassinations and, more unusually, for suicides. The choice of the bow as a murder weapon may be related to the fact that among the Greeks of classical antiquity the bow always remained a weapon of secondary importance, and both the

Odysseus slaying the suitors of his wife, Penelope. From a red-figure cup from Tarquinii, fifth century BC

weapon itself and those who used it were always regarded with suspicion and contempt.

Literary references to archery occur frequently, and bows and arrows are often mentioned in the *Iliad* and in the *Odyssey*, although not in a very flattering manner. On two occasions the bows are described, in the *Iliad* when Pandaros attempted to murder Menelaos and when Odysseus slew the suitors. Because of this disregard we can assume that the Greeks were not particularly interested in developing the bow, and the evidence points to the fact that no particular innovations in bow design were made by the Greeks. This is supported by knowledge of the various bow types that were used in Greece, of which all can be found in other bow-using nations. This situation would occur as a natural effect as foreign mercenaries brought with them their own weapons.

Alexander the Great inherited the throne of Macedonia from his father Philip II in 336 BC, together with a plan for unifying the Greek states so that the Persian Empire could be invaded with their help as revenge for the desecration of Greece by Persia in the fifth century. But that was not all that Alexander inherited. Philip's army and his military ideals were a basis for Alexander's future achievements.

31

The regular Macedonian army was supplemented by contingents raised from subject and allied peoples, the most important being the Thessalian heavy cavalry, the Thracian lancers, the Agrianian javelin-men and, not least of all, the Cretan archers. Alexander was the first general to integrate fully his light troops with other arms; they proved devastating against the Persian chariots, and in mountain campaigns against tribesmen. Alexander himself usually led two squadrons of crack troops, cavalry and infantry, formed as a royal guard; at other times he personally commanded the archers, and it is known that he himself used the bow.

One example of Alexander's brilliant generalship was prior to his Asian campaign, when he decided to quell the Thracians who were causing trouble on one of his frontiers. His force reached a narrow defile where they met the Thracians, who had every intention of stopping his advance. The enemy had assembled a number of heavy carts on high ground which they planned to send crashing down onto the Macedonians with the hope that the impact of the heavy vehicles would cause havoc among the closely packed troops. Alexander could not retreat, so he gave orders to break ranks where possible to let the vehicles through harmlessly. Those sections which were trapped in the narrow pass were to form in the closest possible order, lying prone on the ground with their shields locked together over them so as to give the lumbering wagons a chance to run over the top without doing any harm. There were no casualties; the Macedonians went on to charge the enemy and Alexander brought his archers into position to cover the advancing infantry. The result was a victory for Alexander.

Another ruse employed by Alexander was used against the Triballians, who had taken cover in woods from where they were prepared to fight. Alexander was quick to see that this would have given them the advantage as the local tribesmen knew the terrain and could harass Alexander's forces from that cover. Accordingly he formed his infantry in column and placed his archers ahead, shooting to draw the enemy from the shelter of the trees into open ground. The tribesmen, once they felt the effect of the missiles, came surging forward to get to grips with the lightly armed Macedonian archers, whereupon they were attacked on each flank by the cavalry and at the centre by the infantry. According to Ptolemy the casualties were 3,000 of the

A Persian archer takes aim in a battle against the Macedonians. From the so-called Sarcophagus of Alexander at Sidon, Phoenicia (c.330–320 BC)

32

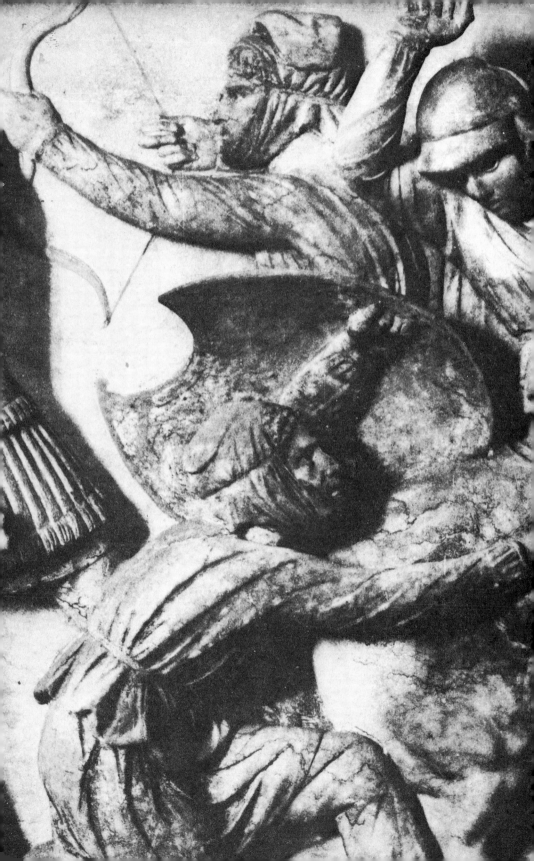

enemy killed against eleven cavalrymen and about forty Macedonian infantry.

These two examples, among many others, illustrate the importance given to the archers in Alexander's army, and also give a brief insight into the brilliant approach and decisive tactics he employed. His challenge to Darius for the throne of Persia had been preceded by the conquering of Syria and Egypt and the assembling of a mighty army of 40,000 foot soldiers, 7,000 horse, Greek mercenaries, Agrianian javelin-men, Thessalian cavalry and, of course, his own Macedonian archers. For twenty months Darius had attempted to build up a respectable army, but it lacked cohesion—the famous Persian archers no longer existed, and the methods of warfare by which the empire had been won in the sixth century had long since been abandoned.

The two armies met to enact the battle of Gaugamela, in 331 BC, Alexander's dispositions heralding Napoleon's battle principle of 'a well-reasoned and extremely circumspect defensive, followed by rapid and audacious attack'. The course of the battle is a matter of historic record, and the consequences were far-reaching. It uncovered the heart of the Persian Empire and made Alexander master of Asia. Gaugamela is acknowledged to be one of the world's greatest battles, and it confirmed the indispensable nature of each specialist in a well co-ordinated military force. In particular, it demonstrated the value of the bow as a weapon of special versatility.

CHAPTER 2

The Barbarians

Throughout the early history of archery in warfare the bow provides a connection between different cultures, a bridge across vast continents, and inextricably links together small tribes and mighty civilizations. No matter what language or environment it provided a common factor; it was a familiar object with an immediately recognizable potential.

Of all the nomad peoples of the steppes in antiquity it is the Scythians, and their successor tribes of Sarmatians and the like, who have won enduring fame. Their sudden move westwards was dramatic and they rapidly dominated the Near East. The Greeks began to know them as a curious and barbaric people from about 600 BC, and so renowned was their archery that Peisistratos seems to have formed a corps of Scythian bowmen in the Athenian army in the later sixth century. They became so redoubtable that even Darius I of Persia failed to destroy their power. They covered vast distances in their raids and perhaps no better witness of the widespread striking power of this warlike tribe could be found than the bronze arrow-heads of Scythian type found in the destruction-levels of hill-forts in Poland on the one hand and, on the other, in the mud walls of the Urartian palace of Karmir Blur in Russian Armenia, 2,000 miles away to the south-east.

The barbed arrow-heads used by the Scythians and the Parthians are masterpieces of the bronze-caster's art. Metal had been used for arrow-heads for centuries; for instance, copper was used for arrow-heads and other weapons in

Mesopotamia and Egypt until it was replaced in about 2000 BC by bronze, a harder alloy of copper and tin. Weapons improved as knowledge of metals and metal-working increased, and gradually beautifully fashioned arrow-heads of cast bronze were produced over a wide area of Asia Minor, provided with a socket to receive the end of the arrow-shaft and three blades, often barbed, coming together in a sharp point. Others were flat, blade-shaped points, and some had two barbs or one vicious 'spur'.

During twenty centuries before Christ the composite bow developed as the dominant weapon in the constant sway of power between the kingdoms of the early civilizations. This weapon, which had found its way to Greece during the early part of the first millennium BC at a period contemporaneous with the foremost period of its use by the Assyrians, also found its way into Italy at about the same time. The Etruscans emerged from the complex ethnic pattern of Iron-Age Italy as a distinct people in about the eighth century BC. From central Italy the Etruscan cities extended their dominion to the north as far as the Reno and Po valleys, and in Campagnia, in the south, flourishing centres sprang up such as Capua, Pompeii, Sorrento and Salerno. The Etruscans played an immensely important rôle in the history of western civilization. We owe to them the diffusion of writing by means of the alphabet they had themselves borrowed from the Greeks, and much of the civilization of Rome was founded on Etrusco-Italic beginnings.

A variety of bronze arrow-heads from Mesopotamia. The earlier forms were flat with short tangs. Later types were provided with well-formed tangs, central ribs and longer blades

The more superior mercenary mounted archers in the Roman armies were probably used as shock troops. This detail from Trajan's column of the first century AD puts emphasis on the bow as a powerful weapon

The peak period of this civilization was the sixth and early fifth centuries BC, but in the middle of the fifth century a decline set in, possibly due to a series of military defeats that Etruria suffered at the hands of her neighbours. In 504 BC land communications with Etruscan Campagnia were cut when the Latins, helped by Aristodemus of Cumae, defeated an Etruscan army at the battle of Aricia. Thirty years later Etruscan sea-power received a crippling blow from allied Greek naval forces off Cumae (474 BC). And finally the southern outposts of Etruria were conquered by the Sammites—Italic mountain tribes from the Apennines—whose invasion of Campagnia culminated in the overthrow of Capua in 423 BC. After this, Etruscan independence was virtually at an end. The Etruscans undoubtedly borrowed the composite bow from the Greeks, and there is reasonable evidence to show that it was used by horsed archers of the Etruscan armies during the height of their power.

The Roman domination at the beginning of the first Punic War in 264 BC did not extend beyond Italy. At the end of that war, in 214, the Carthaginians were turned out of Sardinia and Corsica and from the western half of Sicily, the eastern half continuing under the rule of Syracuse, a Greek settlement allied to Rome. Carthage, which had been traditionally founded exactly 100 years before Rome by the

Phoenicians of Tyre, was called Poeni or Puni by the
Romans, and was therefore Semitic, so it seems safe to
assume that the composite bow contributed largely to the
power of this persistent rival of Rome. The Romans had
a prejudiced attitude towards archery which sprang from
their view that battles, preferably heroic, should be fought
hand-to-hand, and employing others to carry out less presti-
gious tasks was the logical outcome. Another possible
reason for the Roman disdain was the fact that the bow
was not a traditional weapon, or it may have been that the
inferiority of skill or equipment, or both, made the average
archer of very little use. Even more likely is that the Romans
regarded archery as a specialized branch of fighting and
thought that the use of professionals was necessary, such
as those from Crete and Syria. However, eventually, they
acknowledged the usefulness of the bow in war, as Vegetius

*Foot archers in
the Roman army.
The* Cohors
Sagittariorum *were
mercenaries recruited
from countries of the
Mediterranean shores,
where archery had
been perfected for
war. Trajan's column,
first century AD*

commented; 'Cato showed clearly in his books on military training what a great advantage archers have in battles.' The history of the use of the bow in early Roman warfare is more or less restricted to the use of archer-mercenaries employed by the Empire, later to become organized into permanent *auxilia* battalions.

The beginning of the second Punic War was marked by three disastrous engagements for the Romans. After the first, at Trebia, preparations were made for the next campaign which included an appeal for help to Hiero, king of Syracuse, who 'sent a thousand archers and slingers, a force well adapted to cope with Moors and Baliares and other tribes which fought with missiles. . . .' As far as we can tell, the subsequent engagement at Trasumenus on 21 June, 217 BC saw the début of the archer in the Roman forces, although they were not mentioned in reports of the débâcle that followed when Flaminius lost his force of 25,000 soldiers, who were either killed, drowned or taken prisoner.

These Cretan mercenaries, armed with the composite bow, were the first of a long series of foreign bowmen and other troops to be employed by the Romans. There were archers among the Roman attackers and the Sicilian defenders at the siege of Syracuse in 211; mercenary archers provided a substantial proportion of the complement of sixty quinqueremes attacking Achradina from the sea; and, in 207, 3,000 archers were sent to Rome from Sicily, to name but a few instances.

It is not just a question of being an accurate shot that makes a good archer—there are other equally important matters, particularly on the battlefield. A properly trained bowman, in the same way as a properly trained rifleman, will have been taught to care for his personal armament and to be able to cope with unexpected incidents in the heat of battle, which might mar the performance of his weapon.

Assyrian mounted bowmen dispersing camel-riding Arabs. The Arab archers are using simpler bows than the more sophisticated weapons used by the Assyrians

In the preliminary skirmish of the decisive battle against Antiochus III, who was trying to recover Greece, at Magnesia in 189 BC, Rome had probably never before had to face so many bowmen. The cosmopolitan enemy, among all the other regiments, consisted of 1,200 mounted Dahae, 2,500 Mysians, 4,000 Elymaens, and an uncertain number of Arabs on dromedaries who carried six-foot swords. There were 3,000 light infantry, equally divided between Cretans and Trallianians, but we are not told about their weapons. The centre of the Roman battle-line was the regular triple formation of *hastati*, *principes* and *triarii*. The left flank was lightly guarded as it was protected by the river, and the right wing was commanded by King Eamenes II of Pergamum, on the extreme tip of which he stationed 500 Cretans and the same number of Trallianians. The curious thing is that the relatively few Roman auxiliaries seem to have had more success than the masses of the enemy. We are told that the moist fog did not interfere with the Roman view of their own forces in close formation, nor did it affect swords and spears. On the other hand it upset the Antiochene vision of their widely extended troops and 'the moisture had softened the bows and the slings and the thongs of the javelins'. Evidently the Roman allies had spare strings or had taken better care of their weapons in the damp, as Eumenes ordered his Cretan archers, his slingers and dart throwers to shower missiles on Antiochus' chariots. 'The noise and wounds stampede the horses, but the lightly armed Romans easily avoid the counter-charges.'

The third Punic War, 416 BC, started when Carthage attacked Numidia, also an ally of Rome, and ended with the utter destruction of Carthage itself. Within little more than three hundred years, the whole of the Mediterranean and half of Europe was swallowed up by Rome. Julius Caesar seldom alludes to archers in his Gallic War—whether his own or those of his enemies—and he first mentions them in connection with his campaign of 57 BC against the Belgae. 'Using again as guides the men who had come from Iccius to report, Caesar sent off into the middle of the night Numidian and Cretan archers and Balearic slingers to reinforce the townsfolk. . . .' We are directly informed of archers in the reconnaissance of Britain in 55 BC. At first the Britons had the advantage, through light equipment and familiarity, and kept Caesar at bay. He then ordered the

An unfinished drawing which illustrates the near-acrobatic achievement of shooting backwards over the rump of a horse whilst at full gallop—the famed 'Parthian Shot'

galleys containing the missiles 'to row at speed, and to bring up on the exposed flank of the enemy, and to drive and clear them off with slings, arrow and artillery'. After this came the famous jump of the eagle-bearer of the Tenth: Britain had been invaded.

The damage caused by an arrow can vary from a light scratch to instant death, but possibly it was the painful rankling wounds from deeply imbedded barbed arrows which caused the greatest casualties in battle. An early illustration of the result of such wounding was given by Livy in his account of the battle of Mount Olympus between Romans and Gauls: 'Arrows, sling-bullets, darts coming from all sides, wounded them unexpectedly, nor did they think of what to do as their minds were blinded by rage and fear, and they were involved in a kind of battle for which they were very ill-adapted . . . when the sting of a arrow that has buried itself in the flesh torments them, and as they search for a way to extract the missile, it does not

41

come out; turning to madness and shame at being destroyed by so small a thing, throw their bodies on the ground.'

The 10,000 horsed archers of the Parthians at the battle of Carrhae in 53 BC are of more importance than the 500 of the Romans. The Parthian dynasty of Iran was founded by two brothers, leaders of the Parni, who came into northern Iran from the steppe between the Caspian and the Aral about 250 BC. They gradually overcame the Seleucid successors of Alexander and ruled a large empire until they were overthrown by the Sassanids in AD 224. Though they were always regarded as aliens, the Parthians protected the centre of Iran from later nomadic invasions, and fought, often successfully, against the Romans. Typical of their tactics was fast horse-riding through the enemy, rapidly shooting on the move and delivering the 'Parthian Shot' backwards over the rump of the horse.

Crassus, the Roman commander at Carrhae, had 35,000 infantry in seven legions, but poor cavalry. Surenas, the Parthian general, had a few armoured cavalry besides his shooters, but no infantry. The Roman forces were drawn up into a hollow square. At first the depth of the formation, the interlocked shields of the Romans, and the firm composure of the legions deterred the enemy cavalry from charging with their long spears; they seemed to disperse, but quietly surrounded the hollow square. Plutarch now takes up the story: 'And when Crassus ordered his light-armed troops to make a charge, they did not advance far, but encountered a multitude of arrows, abandoned their undertaking and ran back for shelter among the men-at-arms, among whom they caused the beginning of disorder and fear, for they now saw the velocity and force of the arrows, which fractured armour, and tore their way through every covering alike, whether hard or soft.

'But the Parthians now stood at long intervals from one another and began to shoot their arrows from all sides at once, not with any accurate aim (for the dense formation of the Romans would not suffer an archer to miss his man even if he wished it), but making vigorous and powerful shots from bows which were large and mighty and curved so as to discharge their missiles with great force. At once, then, the plight of the Romans was a grievous one; for if they kept their rank, they were wounded in great numbers, and if they tried to come to close quarters with the enemy

A graffito showing a Parthian archer shooting an arrow whilst on the move. Palmyra's caravans were defended by a famous body of similar cavalrymen, some of whom served in the Roman army in Britain

they were just as far from effecting anything and suffered just as much. For the Parthians shot as they fled, and next to the Scythians, they do this most effectively; and it is a very clever thing to seek safety while still fighting, and to take away the shame of flight.

'Now as long as they had hopes that the enemy would exhaust their missiles and desist from battle or fight at close quarters, the Romans held out; but when they perceived that many camels laden with arrows were at hand, from which the Parthians who first encircled them took a fresh supply, then Crassus, seeing no end to this, began to lose heart, and sent messages to his son with orders to force an engagement with the enemy before he was surrounded.' But young Publius fared no better; the Parthians, who appeared to retreat, wheeled round and stirred up the dust so that the Romans could neither see nor speak, but, 'being crowded into a narrow compass and falling one upon another, were shot, and died no easy nor speedy death. For, in the agonies of convulsive pain, and writhing about the arrows, they would break them off in their wounds, and

43

then in trying to pull out by force the barbed heads which had pierced their veins and sinews, they tore and disfigured themselves more. Thus many died, and the survivors also were incapacitated for fighting. And when Publius urged them to charge the enemy's mail-clad horsemen, they showed him that their hands were riveted to their shields and their feet nailed through and through to the ground, so that they were helpless either for fight or self-defence.'

This extensive extract from Plutarch sets out the effects of archery in battle in vivid detail, in addition to providing a wealth of information concerning methods of containing an enemy by the weight of arrow-fire helped by deceptive cavalry tactics. Powerful as the Parthian bow seems to have been it was the 'never-failing quiver' that really won the day. The replenishment of missiles by camel train, just at the critical moment of battle, must have been carefully planned by what could be termed experts in logistics, who were capable of dealing with military supply on a large scale. The rate of shooting a bow can be surprisingly fast—about ten roughly aimed shots a minute would not be unreasonable. If volleys were to be maintained over a period in order to wear down an enemy, then vast quantities of missiles would be required. An archer cannot carry an unlimited supply of arrows; the Egyptians, for example, carried about thirty, and if the same were true of the Parthians, they could have maintained a three-minute barrage. If we presume that at least fifteen minutes of arrow-shot would have to be maintain to demoralize and soften an enemy—probably a conservative estimate—then each archer would require 150 arrows, and accordingly the 10,000 Parthians at Carrhae would have required no less than one and a half million! These are impressive figures, particularly when one considers the organization needed to manufacture these items, apart from their distribution for one battle of many. Records of later periods of European history confirm the scale of such production, particularly in Britain.

The devastation caused by arrows was considerable, but no less effective was the psychological impact. The chroniclers of ancient history frequently speak of the fear that an arrow-storm could provoke in the enemy. There is a logical reason for this particular phenomenon; whereas soldiers in battle can brace themselves to, say, an advance of infantry armed with sword and spear—a positive danger which can readily be observed, anticipated and suitably countered—the unexpected posed less of a positive threat and was therefore more difficult to combat. The suddenness of massed arrows raining down from who knows where must have been no less than terrifying, particularly if, as in the case of Carrhae and other battles, each barrage consisted of tens of thousands of arrows in one great hissing and thudding cloud. At the siege of Dyrrachium the discomfiture of the Caesarians was recorded: '... a great dread of the arrows falling on them, and to avoid the missiles nearly all of the soldiers had made themselves jerkins or other protections out of felt, quilt or hide....' Even metal was no positive protection—'and when the shield of the centurian Scaera was brought to him [Caesar] 120 holes were found in it'.

Without support from cavalry and men-at-arms, and without a sound tactical plan, the *sagittae* were ineffectual once their arrow supplies had dried up, and in later campaigns the pilum and sword became the superior weapons of the Romans. Over two centuries or more there is a wealth of examples of foreign archers being employed in Roman battles, but in fact we know very little about them. We are usually informed of their nationality, sometimes of their numbers, but seldom can we be sure about their status, whether they were allies, mercenaries or conscripts. At the beginning of the Empire, Augustus organized these irregular non-Italic soldiers into permanent *auxilia*, consisting of battalions of infantry, *cohortes*, or wings of cavalry, *alae*. The units consisted of 500 to 1,000 men, and they were usually designated by a number and a special name indicating the man who first enrolled the unit, the nationality of the troops that originally composed it, or the type of equipment used. For example 'I Hamiorum' was a *Cohors Sagittariorum* stationed in Britain during AD 124 to 169, while 'Cohors II Classica' served in Syria, 'Cohors Palmyreni Hadriani' in Egypt, and so on.

During the first few centuries of the Christian era the Huns and many other bloodthirsty tribes of warlike nomads pursued their widespread depredations, and most of eastern Asia was subjected to the brutality of marauding tribesmen from the steppes. The earliest mention of the Huns by a classical writer is thought to be a reference in Ptolemy's *Geography*, a little later than AD 150, to a people called

Chuni, apparently on the Caucasian steppe. This seems to be confirmed by Armenian sources, which report raids from this quarter into western Iran early in the third century AD. Otherwise, western sources say nothing of the Huns until they appear in force in the years following AD 370 to destroy the Gothic power in southern Russia. Their advance deep into Europe precipitated the end of the western Roman Empire; they penetrated western India, which was ruled for a time by Hunnish kings, and they are associated with the empire of the Hsiung Nu, which extended from Korea to the Altai and from the Chinese border to Transbaikalia.

However, it is the western, or Black, Huns who are best known to history, and it is they who represent a warlike group who relied largely on the bow and who used their skills as horsemen to make the archery weapon just about as devastating as it could be. The Hunnish armies overwhelmed the Ostrogoths and the Visigoths, gained control of southern Russia and countries farther east, and made their headquarters in Hungary for operations against the Roman Empire.

When they first reached the Danube valley, the Huns were still a confederacy of their own tribes; to these they began to add non-nomadic German tribes. But they did not have a unified state until this was created for his lifetime by Attila in AD 434. History tells in full the story of Attila the Hun, styled *Flagellum Dei*, the 'Scourge of God'. Chronicles, tales and legends are full of the terror which beset men when the name of the Hun chief was mentioned. Attila himself seems to have been remarkable. There is no lack of descriptions of him; yellower than most of his people, frugal, simple, combining the cruelty and violence of his race with a taste for diplomacy, for legal subtleties, and even for formality. His hordes were made up of Turkestanis, Mongols, Kalmucks and Buriats, and men from tribes of the Herules, the Gepids, the Scyri, the Lombards, the Rugians, the Goths and a dozen other nations now lost in time. These dark, squat riders, with their high cheekbones and narrow eyes, penetrated from the eastern end of Asia across the Urals, and swept unchecked to the gates of Rome. The Huns depended on their tremendous rate of missile discharge for the majority of their victories, and they were quite content to sit the saddle facing the enemy, discharging clouds of arrows and howling uncouth war cries.

46

Their horses gave them a mobility that was never successfully challenged, and these factors, coupled with the psychological advantage of surprise, made them an almost invincible force which would be hard to match throughout human history. This was the terror which inspired the prayer *A sagittis Hunorum, nos defende, Domine*—'From the arrows of the Huns, O Lord, defend us.'

In March 451 Attila, followed by 70,000 warriors and their families, crossed the Rhine and drove the terrified Germans before him, for the brutality of the Asiatic hordes had not been forgotten in Gaul. Metz fell, and Troyes, Paris and Orleans. Rome feared for her survival and the Roman general Aëtius was determined to make a last effort to turn back the floodtide. He had been for a while at Attila's court and understood his methods of warfare. He hurried north, rallying Burgundi, Franks, and Visigoths. During the summer of 451, Attila retired along the Roman road from Orleans towards Troyes. It was near Châlons-sur-Marne on the *Campus Mauriacus*, the Catalaunian plains twelve miles west of Troyes, that Aëtius gave battle. This famous event was the most important of all the battles during this period of the invasions, and the one whose consequences were the most lasting.

By now Rome had been sacked more than once, and the legions had been withdrawn from Britain to protect Italy. The barbarians had settled in Roman provinces and her possessions in northern Africa had been lost. The Romans under Aëtius desperately wanted to drive off this latest powerful threat from Attila. In the event the Romans defeated the Huns, although nothing certain is known of the battle except that it was 'savage and tenacious, complex and vast'—but we may be sure that thousands of casualties were caused through the archery of the Hunnish hordes. Attila was again checked when he invaded Italy the following year by help from natural allies of Rome—famine and disease, in addition to imperial reinforcements and the Pope's diplomacy. The year after that Attila took a new wife and died as a result of a blood-vessel burst during his wedding night. As Chaucer commented later:

Loke, Attila the grete conquerour,
Deyde in his sleep, with shame and dishonour,
Bledinge ay at the nose in drokenesse,
A capitayn shoulde live in sobrenesse.

Attila's sudden death in AD 453 forestalled a grand attack on the East Roman Empire and brought his system and the unified power of the Huns to a premature end. The Hunnish Empire was broken up by dynastic quarrels and rebellion of subject peoples, particularly the Germans. The defeat of the Huns and the death of Attila did not save Rome. A struggle for power in the now weakened Empire, split East and West, began, and Africa, Spain and Italy were subjected to twenty years of conflict, which itself heralded a new era of warfare characterized by the heavy-armed knight and his retainers.

Before and under Attila, the Hunnish domination consisted of central territories held by the Huns in varying strength, and a ring of lands occupied by subject peoples under obedient chiefs or Hunnish governors. Archaeology has revealed fairly clear traces of Hunnish rule. Burials of local chiefs in the outlying regions have yielded, among more usual treasures and weapons, a number of gold plates of curious shape. It is now believed that they were gilding plates for ceremonial bows which would have been emblems of Hunnish authority. Some of the bows were evidently of full size and their plates would have applied only to the unbending middle section; these could have been real weapons, however ornate. Others were smaller and must, from the shape of the plates, have been gilded from end to end; these would have been purely ceremonial objects. Such bow plates have been found, for example, at Pecsüszög in Hungary, Jakuszowice in Poland, and far away east at such places as Novogrigoryevko on the Dniepr and Vorovoye on the Tobol in northern Kazakhstan.

Throughout their turbulent history the Romans found themselves facing adversaries armed with the composite bow. It was used by the Etruscans and the Latins in the early struggles with the Romans, and it was carried by the barbarian tribesmen during their invasions of the Roman colonies. In their capture of Mesopotamia from the Parthians and their involvement in the Persian War, where they were faced with archers on camels, as well as in their actions against the Goths and during the ravages of the Huns in Europe, the Roman armies must have realized the potentiality of such a common weapon, and its dire effectiveness must repeatedly have been demonstrated to them.

Marcus Aurelius in 175 was the first to regard weekly

archery practice for the archer-battalions of the Roman armies as a serious matter. These were organized sessions where a set drill was laid down, with standards to be achieved and even rewards to be gained. According to Vegetius in the fourth century AD there seemed to be a great increase in the use of archery, although this may have been somewhat exaggerated. In his military text-book, among other matters, he included a recommendation that at least a quarter of the recruits should be trained as archers: 'The youngest and fittest should be exercised at the post with wooden bows and target arrows.' Vegetius was not alone in advocating the wider use of the bow by the Romans. Saint Leo the Great, during whose papacy Attila was defeated at Châlons-sur-Marne in 452 by the Roman general Aëtius, also emphasized the importance of the bow, and attempted, rather belatedly and ineffectually, to introduce it officially to the armed forces other than the *auxilia*. In his *Military Constitutions* he says: 'You shall command all Roman youth, till they come to forty years of age, whether they have mean skill in shooting or not, to carry bows and quivers of arrows. For since the art of shooting hath been neglected, many and great losses have befallen the Romans,' and in another place, '. . . but specially you are to have care of archers; and they that who remain at home, and have vacation from war, hold bows and arrows in their houses. For carelessness herein hath brought great damage to the Roman state.' The same theme is echoed in later European history where the power of the bow was experienced, half-heartedly taken up, and then neglected.

The Romans allowed archery to decline, and the bow gradually became a plaything for nobility instead of being a weapon in times of war. The Byzantine Emperor Leo V (813–820), Flavius the Armenian, restating the plea of the first pope of that name, said: 'Let all the youth of Rome be compelled to use shooting and always bear their bow and their quiver until they be eleven years old . . . for the leaving off of shooting has brought in ruin and decay the whole empire of Rome.' Whereas Leo's assertion is hard to believe, it is true that the Romans never really accepted the bow as a natural weapon.

The wars which dragged down Rome produced one outstanding general: Belisarius. The Byzantine army had for some time been adapting itself to be able to compete in the

49

new era of Gothic warfare. It was formed almost entirely out of mercenaries from the various barbarian tribes, and consisted mostly of cavalry, with a few units of heavy infantry. In the 520s Belisarius set about training an élite corps of heavy cavalry armed with both bow and lance, trained to be skirmishers as well as shock troops. He also armed them with feathered darts, which were thrown by hand at close quarters. Finally, in case everything else should fail, they carried a heavy broadsword. It required a lot of skill to become proficient with all four weapons and to be able to control a horse at the same time. Since two hands were needed to use the bow, Belisarius trained his men to support themselves in the saddle by the stirrups and to control the movements of the horse with their knees. The men had a small shield strapped to the left arm, and wore sleeveless mail shirts of thigh length and tall boots of rawhide. When not in use the bow was slung over the shoulder; the arrows were kept in a quiver next to the broadsword on the left thigh, and twelve darts were carried in a receptacle attached to the shield, while the lance was carried in a leather bucket on the right side. The archery methods were copied from the Huns, and tilting with the lance from the Goths. The training exercise to improve the skill of the knight was to gallop towards a stuffed dummy hanging from a gallows. The rider had to string his bow as he approached, shoot three arrows at the swaying figure, and finish the charge with lance or darts. Pay, rations and rank were awarded according to proficiency in this and other exercises.

Belisarius had learnt his profession in operations on the Danube and in the east. For example, against the Hunnic mounted archers of Bulgaria he devised an original and successful tactic. The problem was to come to close quarters with them; his solution was to tempt them with live bait— a few men on swift horses, who would draw the eager Huns into a position where their retreat could be cut off. To deal with the wagon barricades, Belisarius ordered his men to ride to windward of them and set them alight with incendiary arrows, an example of utilizing the full potential of carefully aimed missiles which was repeated again and again in later centuries. Belisarius successfully waged war against the Vandals, and conquered the Ostrogoths in Italy. He gave a new concept to the multi-national armies of mer-

This is a stance which could be used most effectively with short composite bows, probably shooting from low cover. A Roman representation of Hercules (c.490 BC)

50

cenaries; in a sense he had created what could be termed the first feudal army, which succeeded against the loose-knit hordes of allied tribesmen, however well they were led.

The use of the bow to project missiles of a non-lethal variety was a facility employed from time to time in ancient history, and several ingenious applications have been recorded. A curious book was published in 1694 which collected together examples of 'the swiftness of conveyance by Bodies, whether Inanimate, as Arrows, Bullets; or Animate, as Man, Beasts, Birds'. In this book, *Mercury, or the Secret and Swift Messenger*, the author, no less than the Bishop of Chester, gives several instances of 'fastening a writing to an arrow' which are of particular interest. In about 480 BC, for example, Artabazus and Timoxenus, 'when they could not come together were wont to inform one another of any things that concerned their affairs, by fastening a letter unto an Arrow, and directing it to some appointed place, where it might be received.' The conditions of this arrangement are not so precisely recorded as those of the incident during the siege of Troezen, in 279 BC, when Cleonymus, a prince of Lacedaemon, 'injoyned the Soldiers to shoot several Arrows into the Town, with notes fastened unto them having this inscription, "I come that I may restore this place to its Liberty", upon which the credulous and discontented Inhabitants were very willing to let him enter.' These 'liberation' messages can be likened to the propaganda pamphlets used by both Allied and German forces in the Second World War as a subtle form of psychological warfare. Another instance, mentioned by the Rev. Wilkins, was the use of such messages to raise morale by specific strategic information. When Cicero was besieged by the Gauls in 54 BC, his forces were on the point of yielding. Unknown to him reinforcements were hastening to his aid. To persuade him to hold out until help arrived Caesar ordered an arrow to be shot into the city with the message *Caesar ciceroni fiduciam optat, expecta auxilian*—'Caesar requires Cicero to have confidence, help is coming.' The message had the desired effect and the day was saved.

But perhaps the most curious of all messaged arrows was that which was shot by Aster of Amphipolis, which put out the eye of Philip of Macedonia, the father of Alexander, during the siege of Methone in 354 BC. It bore the magical message: 'Aster sends this deadly shaft against Philip.'

CHAPTER 3

Saracens and Tartars

The Byzantine Empire was founded by Constantine in AD 330, when he dedicated as a new capital for the Roman Empire the fabulously rich city of Byzantium, renamed Constantinople, later to become Istanbul. The faith that Rome had persecuted was the binding force that enabled the reorganized Roman Empire, with its new capital in the east, to survive for more than 1,100 years, long after the Roman Empire in the west had perished. It owed its traditions of law and government to Rome and its language and learning to Greece, and the emperor Constantine was shrewd enough to see that Christianity, with its power to sway the minds of men and harness their loyalty, was the one force that could save the empire. He also saw that Rome, as well as being a centre of intrigues and feuds, was far too steeped in the older pagan beliefs to be suitable as a capital of a Christian empire.

This was the religious tinder-box which sparked off disputes, eventually leading to the rift between Western Christianity and Eastern (Orthodox) Christianity which lasts to this day; an uneasy peace which from time to time foments into bloody conflict. The causes of the Crusades were essentially a conflict between shades of faith, which degenerated finally to sending fellow Christians to eternity for the baser reasons of greed and power.

Civil war broke out almost immediately after Constantine's death in 337, and the empire was assailed in turn by Goths, Huns, Persians, Avars, Bulgars, Slavs, Vikings, Arabs, Berbers, Turks, Crusaders and Normans. All these

A river battle during the Viking invasion of Russia. The use of archery was clearly an important feature of this engagement in the fourteenth century

invaders were armed with the bow, most with the composite variety and some, such as the Vikings and Normans, to a lesser extent with the long self-wood bow. To defend the vast possessions of this empire Byzantium had not only good leaders, but thousands of tough, enthusiastic men settled in the frontier areas with obligations to provide armies. For many years, as many as 100,000 men were serving at one time, stimulated by two incentives—loot and the glory to be had from recovering Christian lands. The

54

heavy cavalry which Belisarius took so much trouble to train was the component of the Byzantine armies which provided the main strength for the rest of that empire's history. Like its Roman predecessors, and unlike any other Western army before the sixteenth century, the Byzantine army can be said to have worn uniform; the surcoat, the lance-pennon and the tuft of the helmet were of a particular colour for each unit.

The functions of the infantry were limited to the defence of defiles and mountainous country, and the garrisoning of fortresses and important cities. However, when one considers the vast frontiers of this empire, their task was enormous. Most of the light infantry were archers, though some were javelin-men. The bowman sometimes wore a mail shirt, but more often only a tunic and stout boots. Besides his bow, he carried a quiver containing forty arrows, an axe at his belt should he have to engage the enemy at close quarters, and a small round buckler which could be slung over his back. Like the cavalry, the infantry had a considerable body of camp followers. For every unit of sixteen men, two carts carried reserves of arrows and food, cooking utensils and entrenching tools—spades, mallets, axes and saws. Every unit of 400 men had a medical unit including stretcher-bearers. The bearers were paid a bonus for every casualty brought in from the battlefield—not for humanitarian reasons, but because the state was interested in restoring the wounded to battle fitness as soon as possible.

A large proportion of the Byzantine army consisted of mercenaries, but these decreased after Justinian's wars. Despite the efforts of several emperors there was no universal male conscription in the empire, but a system which called on every estate to send a certain number of men for training and active service when required. The best professional soldiers came from Cappadocia, Isaura and Thrace.

The keynote of the Byzantine military system was impressive tactical organization; they fought cunningly and efficiently. Their battle theory was built up from the basic military principle of delivering a series of heavy cavalry charges with support from archers on the wings and infantry to close in after the cavalry. There were, naturally, many variations on tactical disposition and the Byzantines rightly considered that the methods to be employed in battle must be varied according to the tactics of their opponents. Their

55

A siege during the Crusades, about 1190. The unfortunate defender pierced by an arrow was probably a VIP. Note also the water-borne attackers armed with bows

strategy was mostly defensive, because they were called on to defend their positions more often than not, and rarely did Byzantium become an aggressive power.

It is interesting to note that different forms of conducting war were worked out by the Byzantine theorists as a match for the predominant characteristics of their many enemies. For example, special instructions were issued about how to deal with the light horsemen of the eastern European and western Asiatic plains, the Bulgars, the Magyars and the

Patzinaks or 'Turks' as they were called. They fought in innumerable small bands, armed principally with the bow,
and they were particularly efficient at scouting and fond of
ambushing. In attack they would dash up and down the
enemy front showering it with volleys of arrows and delivering short stinging charges. To combat these tactics the
Byzantine heavy cavalry was directed to close with the
attackers as quickly as possible, and the foot archers to
engage them promptly; their larger and more powerful
bows outranged the enemy, and if the steppe-fighter lost his
horse he was helpless. Caution was recommended, however,
for careless pursuit by the cavalry would be fatal, since in
Parthian style the Turks liked to rally from simulated flight
and turn on disordered pursuers. Other patterns of tactical
behaviour were worked out according to varied terrain, to
counter different types of weaponry and to overcome other
forms of battle procedure, and these instructions became
a model which proved extremely successful.

The history of the Byzantine Empire continued relentlessly with invasion after invasion. The Arabs won Syria
in 636, Palestine in 638, and Persia and Egypt in 641.
Greece, parts of North Africa, Sicily and southern Italy
were lost by the ninth century, but the fortunes of war

The 'Parthian Shot' was also practised by mounted Turkish archers, as in this fifteenth-century miniature

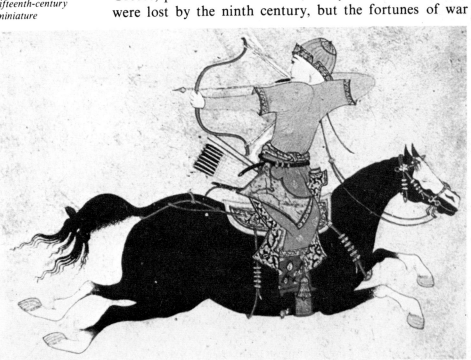

57

turned and the next 200 years saw the return of much of the lost territory. However this was only a temporary recovery because by the beginning of the thirteenth century the empire had shrunk again to a little more than what is now Greece and the western half of Turkey. The supreme tragedy was the invasion of its capital by western European armies which had originally set out on the fourth Crusade for the Holy Land.

The Crusades were carried forward on a wave of religious fervour which began when Pope Urban II called upon Europe to recapture the Holy Land from the Moslems, with the promise that, 'Those who lose their lives in such an enterprise will gain Paradise and the remission of their sins.' The response was tremendous, and in 1096 the first contingents set off from most parts of western Europe to gain the posthumous double honour—or, if they returned, to bring back the plunder of looted citadels. A curious phenomenon had crept into European warfare during the previous three or four hundred years—it had become increasingly involved with religion, and many a battle had been fought in a strange atmosphere of religious exaltation. Some of the outcomes were curious; for example in 1027 a Synod at Elme prohibited all warfare at weekends; in the twelfth century those who accepted the Truce undertook to abstain from fighting for three-quarters of the year, under pain of excommunication; and the strangest of all, the Lateran Council in 1139 forbade the use of the crossbow—except against infidels—as being a weapon too murderous for 'Christian warfare'! During the Crusades the foundations of chivalry were laid with a heavy emphasis on the religious and social aspects, and knighthood developed into a kind of fraternity embraced by a new religious order with its own special codes of behaviour.

This, then, was the background of the Holy Wars, which lasted 200 years, originally to set up Christian rule in Palestine. Later, Egypt and Constantinople became targets for attack, and in the fourteenth century the conquests of the Ottoman Turks turned crusading into a defensive movement. The greatest majority of peoples involved during this period were users of the bow in war, as was the case in one of the more spectacular battles of the Crusades, the Battle of Arsuf, fought between Richard I and Saladin in the year 1191. This was one of the longest and hardest-fought battles of the Crusades, where the bowmen on either side bore the brunt of the engagement.

The main striking power of the Saracens lay with their mounted archers from various Turkic tribes who, apart from their skill with the bow, were brilliant horsemen and could use lance, sword or mace with equal adroitness. Their basic tactic against the Crusaders was to harass them at relatively long range with the bow, their cavalry sweeping past at full gallop. Pressure would later be increased and the range closed with the object of forcing a gap in the ranks of infantry. When this was achieved, bows were slung over their shoulders and the gap was charged using sword or mace for close combat. The Crusaders' defence was to present a wall of shields, behind which archers and cross-bowmen strove to keep Saracens at long range. Behind them came the mounted knights waiting their chance to move forward in a massive and overwhelming charge.

Problems of supply were always present in unfamiliar country, and often with long lines of communication the transportation of reserves of materials, such as arrow replenishments, always presented special challenges. Such a challenge had been successfully met by Saladin, who had 400 loads of arrows in his main baggage train, with seventy camels to bring up reserves for the close support of his mounted archers so that horsemen could replenish their quivers after each attack.

After the successful siege of Acre, King Richard began a march along the coast towards Jaffa, which was to be his main base for future operations against Jerusalem. He set out with an army of 100,000, with every move observed and reported by Saracen scouts. Saladin kept ahead and a little inland. Well-wooded slopes just outside Arsuf were selected by Saladin as a suitable battlefield area, but Richard wasn't to be provoked into an early engagement and continued to move onwards towards Jaffa. Closest to the shore came the baggage train, then the knights and, farthest inland, the infantry and archers, presenting a long vulnerable flank to the Saracens. They wore heavy hauberks, long coats of mail, with thick quilted gambesons beneath, which must have been unbearable in the early September sun.

Richard was determined to keep moving, although his rearguard sustained attack after attack. Baha ed-Din remarked, 'The Turks, skilled in the bow, pressed unceasingly upon them; the air was filled with showers of arrows and the brightness of the sun was obscured by the multitude of missiles as if it had been darkened by a fall of winter's hail or snow.' He then continued, 'The [Christian] foot-men, drawn up in front of the horse, held as firmly as a wall. Each man was clad in a jerkin of thick felt and a coat of mail; I saw some with ten arrows fixed in their backs, yet marching along at their ordinary pace, without quitting their ranks.'

Having reached Saladin's battleground, the main engage-ment began. At the commencement, 'marksmen drawn from each [Saracen] squadron went out in advance and rained a shower of arrows on the enemy'. The use of speci-ally selected archers suggests that purposeful targets were picked out, such as commanders and captains, standard-bearers, the horses of marked noble knights and suchlike, in order to lower morale and create confusion. These soften-ing tactics continued, relates the *Intinerarium* of Richard, until about 'the third hour, when lo! a host of Turks, 10,000 in number, swept rapidly down upon our men, hurling darts and arrows.' Paterson, the expert on Asiatic archery who studied this battle particularly from the technical aspect, concluded that the 'darts' referred to were short arrows shot with the aid of a guide or *majra*. In effect this was an open barrel of wood or bamboo held against the side of the bow along which a dart was projected, a kind of unfixed cross-bow stock, the string being released manually in the ordi-nary way.

The greatest part of the attack which developed at Arsuf was an engagement between the archers on either side. 'That day our losses and the suffering of our horses, who were pierced through and through with arrows and darts, showed how persistently the enemy kept up the attack,' related the English version of the battle, 'and then indeed we found out the use of our stalwart crossbowmen, our bowmen, and those closely wedged followers who at the very rear beat back the Turkish onslaught by constant hurling of their mis-siles as far as they could.' The resistance of Richard's forces began to falter and hand-to-hand fighting broke out, but the day was saved by a spirited charge by the knights, fol-lowed by the cavalry, which began the final phase of the battle. The Saracen line was broken, the Crusaders rallied and fell on the enemy again and again and finally 'drove them in headlong rout right up to the wood at Arsuf....'

The point to be made about this battle, particularly in regard to the part played by the archers, is that the majority of the engagement was an exhausting exchange of arrow shot, which, by sufficiently weakening both sides, meant that a careful judgement of the right moment to move in the heavy cavalry could produce a victory. It is also interesting to note that the initial provocation, which slowed up Richard's march, was produced by a studied plan of sniper action, from which the battle proper began. The chroniclers on both sides, both of whom have been quoted, agree that the battle was a long one, certainly several hours, and to sustain an exchange of archery for such a time needed not only a vast supply of arrows, but also a well-drilled system of replenishment for individual bowmen.

Perhaps a word should be said here about the crossbow. This artifice, as it was once described by toxophilitic purists, is allied to the hand bow by its source of power, but there the similarity ends; it embraces a different technology and has a separate evolutionary pattern. It features often in medieval battles, frequently side-by-side with the more regular type of bow, and it provided a very important item in the weaponry of European and Asiatic armies from an early period. To do full justice to its history would require a companion volume to this, and therefore, somewhat regretfully, it must be left among the other weapons of our story, such as the spear, sword and axe, to supplement our principal intention of describing archery in war through the bow and arrow and those that used it.

Though the Crusades failed in effecting the spiritual objectives for which they were intended, they benefited Europe indirectly in a number of ways. The stimulation of trade between Europe and Asia Minor was perhaps the most important overall aspect, and this embraced the intro- duction of new and rare products from eastern Europe such as sugar, cotton and many other articles now of everyday use. Soldiers learnt valuable lessons from Saracen skills in art and in war, but, somewhat surprisingly, the craft of the Saracen bowyers remained their secret. One would have thought that the use of the composite bow in battle, experi- enced at first hand, would have convinced any military com- mander of the eleventh to the thirteenth centuries that, if it was not already in use by his own armies, it was not only

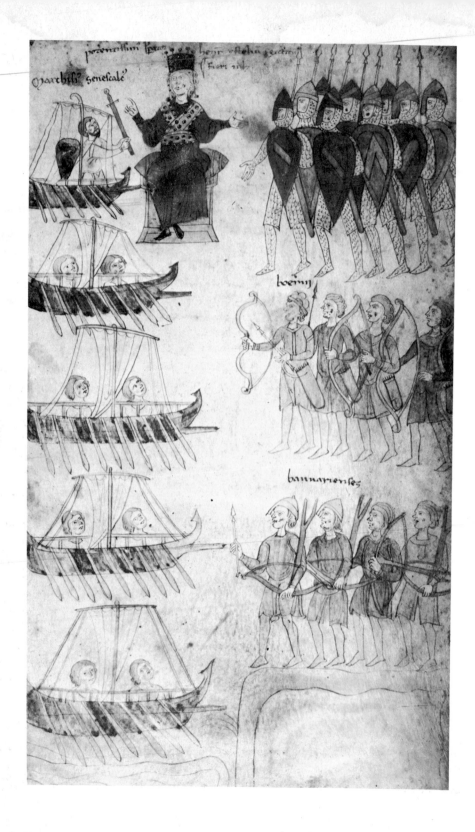

desirable but essential as a long-range weapon. In addition, it had been demonstrated—notably by Saladin—that properly ordered mounted archers in battle could carry the day by their speed and striking power. Yet another advantage was the power of penetration of an arrow shot from a composite bow compared with that shot from a slower and less powerful bow. Quilting, leather and even mail armour were no protection from a deftly aimed arrow.

In their book *Saracen Archery*, Latham and Paterson state that in the Middle East at this time the bow was widely used by the literate, and that the contrary was true in the West. Thus the composite bow, with its intricacies of manufacture, its elaborate method of handling, and even its aesthetic regard as a cult object, must have been a weapon outside the commonplace, and therefore not easily accepted by non-literate soldiers.

Support for the literate theory, which proposes that the composite bow was used by literate civilizations, can be found when contemporaneous archery literature is examined. From as early as the twelfth up to the fourteenth century there are at least ninety-five Arabic, Persian and Turkish manuscripts known, either wholly or partly dealing with archery. Many of these are extremely detailed and they include manuals for war and textbooks for competitive shooting. For example one, written in 1174, is entitled in translation, *Enlightenment for the intelligent on the means of deliverance in warfare*; another, of about 1348, is called *Manual on the art of war and military skills and techniques*; and in 1394 a book that is the subject of *Saracen Archery* has the title, *Essential archery for beginners*, which no doubt was compulsory reading for the Saracen conscript issued with his first bow and quiver of arrows. The fact that it was not until two hundred years or so later that any book on archery appeared in English is significant; as Latham and Paterson commented, 'There would have been little point in writing for the illiterate, from whose ranks the average bowman was drawn.' However, in due course we shall see how the English bowman fared without the benefits of the composite bow and a good education.

Another important clue as to the reason why the skills of archery were so well developed in the early Arab world is the fact that it was regarded as a religious obligation by true followers of Muhammad. There is an authentic tradi-

The Emperor Henry VI, before the conquest of Sicily in the twelfth century. The personal protection of the troops varied with the type of arms they carried. The least well protected were the handbow archers

tion of the Prophet that it is a sin to give up archery after learning the art. There are, furthermore, numerous other traditions of the Prophet which commend archery, and he himself considered that there was no better weapon. There would, accordingly, be every encouragement to become proficient and to emulate the Prophet, who was himself an archer; the bow was therefore an approved weapon, its ownership and use proclaiming a true believer, and its employment in war being almost an act of worship.

Despite the aesthetic and religious connotations that were associated with the bow, it required a great deal of training and practice to become a proficient archer. The Turks that we have referred to were descended from a variety of tribal sources, such as the Khorasanians, from about the ninth century. The courage and martial prowess of these warriors evoked the admiration of contemporaries, who have left impressive accounts of their skill as bowmen and horse-archers. Their military training included boys practising vaulting onto horses' backs and men playing polo, after which came 'shooting at the sitting quarry, the hoop, and the bird on the wing'. The Turkish slave-troops followed, of whom it was written, '... if a thousand of their horse join battle and let off a single bout of arrows, they can mow down a thousand enemy horse.' And again, 'The Turk can shoot at beasts, birds, hoops, men, sitting quarries, dummies, and birds on the wing, and do so at full gallop to fore or to rear, to left or to right, upwards or downwards, loosing ten arrows before the Kharijite can nock one.' The advent of the Seljuks and the creation of the Great Sultanate in 1055 finally established the power of the Turks.

The victory of the Seljuk Turks over the Byzantines at Manzikert in 1071 opened the way for the Turkish advance into Asia Minor. Turkish chieftains and their followers drifted westwards. They were looking for homes, but they were also inspired by their faith as *ghazis*, warriors for the Moslem faith. They obeyed a military and moral code as formal as chivalry, and more dynamic. They acknowledged only in a loose sense the authority of the Seljuk sultan; it therefore made little difference to the western *ghazis*, and did not help Europe at all, when in 1243 the Seljuks were overthrown by the Mongols. The Mongols quickly departed, but their pressure had reinforced the westward

*A fine study of a
Turkish* Janissary, *one
of the regular
professional soldiers of
the Ottoman Empire,
with typical composite
bow and neat quiver of
arrows taking
prominence of place.
By Gentile Bellini,
fifteenth century*

impulse of the Turks. Thus both pressure and faith lured the *ghazis* to attack the tumbledown Byzantine Empire. Soon after the fall of the Seljuks, the Ottomans emerged as leaders of the Turks. This was due initially to their western position, which allowed them to survive the Mongol onslaught and made them a rallying point for other *ghazis*. Europe was in no condition, then or later, to repel the Turkish threat. The end of the political and military power of Byzantium had been signalled by the Crusaders' sack of Constantinople in 1204, and this ruin was completed when western Anatolia, the empire's chief source of manpower and food, was finally lost to the Turks. The Europeans knew that they faced a superior military power, and when they did oppose the Ottoman advance, the depressing experience of the Crusades was confirmed by a succession of resounding defeats.

The soldiers in the Turkish army owed their duty to the sultan as an individual rather than to the state. The military system was comparable to the European feudal system, but it worked a great deal better. The bulk of the army was regu-

65

lar militia, settled on land in return for military service as required. The feudal troops, which were cavalry, constituted the main reliable mass of the army. There were also hordes of irregular troops, infantry called *bashibazouks* and cavalry called *akibi*, who were unpaid and fought for plunder. The élite troops of the Turkish army were the sultan's own corps of guards, the *Janissary* infantry and the *Spahi* cavalry. The *Janissaries* were rightly the most celebrated troops in the Turkish army. They were professional infantry, and the method of their recruitment was extraordinary but, as it turned out, sound. They were taken as children from Christian families, mostly in the Balkan countries, and trained in special communities. They were then affiliated to a religious order of dervishes, and thus received in their monastery-barracks an education which made them fanatical Moslems. They were also given the best physical education possible and were highly trained in the handling of their weapons. At the height of their greatness in the first half of the sixteenth century, the *Janissaries* numbered between 12,000 and 15,000—of which in peacetime about half were stationed in the provinces and half in the capital. Their original weapon was the bow, the short composite weapon which far outranged any other type. To qualify for admission to the archers' guild, founded by Mehmed II, it was necessary to have shot an arrow 630 yards, although the effective range for fighting was much less. The men were not heavily laden with protective armour; they had a small round shield, a metal helmet with a sharp point on top, and possibly some light mail. There were colourful uniforms for each section, and the soldiers wore the emblem of their corps, which for the *Janissaries* was a wooden spoon; they also went in for a lot of tattooing. European observers were impressed by these troops, who were highly trained, well disciplined and imbued with religious zeal and loyalty to their sultan. The bow fell out of favour as soon as the arquebus appeared, although the earlier weapon continued to be carried on ceremonial occasions.

During the Mameluke period from the middle of the thirteenth to the end of the fourteenth century, vast numbers of Turks from the Kipchak steppe and surrounding regions were recruited and formed into corps of archers; about 1,000 were selected to become the Bahriyyah regiment, an élite guard for the sultans. The Kipchaks proved to be

A nomadic rider of the steppes with carefully protected bow ready for instant use, plus an ample supply of arrows

excellent soldiers, and it was they who signally defeated the Mongols in pitched battle in 1260 and checked their advance into Syria and Egypt. The rôle of the bow at this time was important and the skill of the Mameluke archers in their heyday is legendary. Even after the advent of firearms the bow was not hastily cast aside. 'To equip a soldier with an arquebus,' commented Ayalon the Arabic scholar, 'meant taking away his bow and, what was to the Mameluke more distasteful, depriving him of his horse, thereby reducing him to the humiliating status of a foot soldier, compelled either to march or to be carried in an ox-cart.' In their eyes the importance of the bow was such that, in the period of decline, failure to pass tests in its use was used as the criterion for stopping the privileges of members of the non-Mameluke socio-military corps, to which were attached sons of noblemen and Mamelukes debarred by the non-hereditary system of their society from making a career in that group.

We must step back a little in time to take a brief look at a charismatic leader of bowmen-riders of the steppes, whose impact on the history of Asia resounded throughout that continent. Historians coldly eye Jenghiz Khan (about 1162–1227) as a conqueror with a taste more for blood than politics, and for pillage rather than authority. The charges are true. For all his epic military conquests, the Mongol leader left no words for posterity, his people no significant cultural artefacts. Only the cold ashes of gutted cities marked his passing. But if Jenghiz Khan was ruthless, he was also brilliant, a leader whose genius for the martial arts surpassed the best that China, Korea and eastern Europe could throw against him. Seven centuries ago this illiterate son of the steppes conceived tactics which were to remain through the ages. His basic concepts of battle were found eminently sound by Napoleon, were used by Foch and Pershing, and re-employed by Rommel and Patton. Jenghiz Khan was the first to grasp that the horse-mounted archer was almost invincible, if he could somehow overcome the advantages of numbers and better armour which protected his foes. He set out methodically to discipline his wild plunderers, to mould them into a mobile striking force of loyal warriors. He introduced an order of battle and drew up his men into precise squadrons. The idea of war games—training manœuvres in which his men could simulate combat and perfect their field operations—was enforced by the Khan, and he imbued his men with a sense of loyalty and devotion to his banner based on a code of honour—and also on the certainty that a fair share of the women and the booty would fall to their lot.

The Mongol riders carried seventy arrows designed to meet a variety of targets in different battle situations. These included armour-piercing arrows, their points tempered to steely hardness by immersion in salt water while hot; arrow grenades; incendiary arrows; and arrows designed for long-range shots. They even had a special arrow fitted with a head shaped like an open pair of scissors, which it was said, could cut off a man's arm at the point of impact. All these arrows were carried in quivers, divided into compartments and slung at the right side of the saddle, the bow itself being carried in a leather case on the warrior's left. Jenghiz Khan saw in massed arrow-shot a tremendous psychological advantage as well as a powerful military weapon. With the powerful composite bow in the hands of his tough, disciplined and highly trained warriors, the Khan added the only remaining element needed for his plan of conquest—the right tactics. His enemies invariably advanced on a line, and so Jenghiz Khan evolved the wheeling flank attack as the manœuvre best suited to stop them. In an attack the Khan's commanders effectively deployed their men with signal flags; then at the right moment, masterfully, the drilled mounted units would swing round to exploit an enemy's weak point. They would ride in tightly massed ranks, and unleash a deadly cloud of arrows at selected targets identified by carefully directed whistling arrows shot by their leaders. When the enemy lines wavered under the missile attack and their horses were wounded and reeling, the Mongols would rush in with lance, battle-axe and curved short sword. Thus an overwhelming volley of arrows was combined with mobility—in effect, a *blitzkrieg*.

After interminable battles against numerous Tartar tribes, Jenghiz Khan was finally proclaimed Khan of the united Mongol and Tartar peoples. At this juncture, he declared that he had been called by heaven to conquer the world (a declaration which has an all too familiar ring). This implicit belief communicated itself to his troops, and he was able to lead them on from one victory to another. The land of the Uigurs in the middle of central Asia submitted to him voluntarily, and Jenghiz Khan became overlord of all the Tartars. In the year 1211 the mighty Khan led hundreds of thousands of Mongols against the Great Wall of China and, although he stormed the gate forts with ease, it took him five years, aided by an army of 700,000, to conquer China. In 1218 he destroyed the capital of Khwaresm, and had the sultan pursued to India. From 1219 to 1221 his troops passed through central Asia and Turkestan, overthrowing Bokhara, Samarkand (garrisoned by a force of 110,000), Balkh and Merv. During 1221 to 1223 they reached Azerbaijan, Georgia, the Crimea and southern Russia. In 1225 Jenghiz overthrew his neighbours, the Tanguts, and in 1227 he died. The Khan's standard of nine yak tails surmounted by a white falcon was carried victoriously from the Yellow Sea to the Baltic, and to the shores of the Adriatic. The empire, which had been gained with bow and sword, was divided between his four sons.

An example of one less spectacular facet of Jenghiz Khan's character occurred during a battle against the Taichuts, illustrating the shrewdness of the Khan and his ability to turn what would normally have been a minor incident into a practical and political advantage, as well as revealing a surprisingly humane side to his character. When the tide of battle had turned against him, due mainly to internal strife among his own men, Jenghiz was wounded in the neck by an arrow from an enemy archer. One of his closest friends stayed up the whole night tending the wound to try and prevent it festering. He then crawled into the enemy camp and stole some rancid milk, which was considered to be the best medicine. By the following morning Jenghiz had made a miraculous recovery and managed to lead his troops into the battle that finally wiped out the Tai-chuts. Amongst the prisoners taken was the man who had so nearly killed Jenghiz; he stood before his captor and said that if he were killed his body would simply soil a small strip of ground, but if he were allowed to live then Jenghiz would have a good marksman who would help him conquer the world. The appeal must have touched a responsive spark of mercy, for Jenghiz made him one of his commanders and gave him the name of Gebe the Archer. It was through the skills of this man and many other carefully chosen subordinates who were essentially 'drawn from the ranks', that Jenghiz Khan was able to make his conquests.

During the mid-thirteenth century the Mongol forces, which had already driven deep into central Europe, threatened to overrun and obliterate the Christian civilization of the West. Prince Batu, now the supreme commander of the Mongol army and future founder of the Golden Horde, pressed on even further towards realizing the dreams of world conquest which his grandfather, Jenghiz Khan, had pursued so relentlessly. In the summer of 1240 the Mongols, from their bases in the Caucasus area, attacked what was then the southernmost region of Russia, and this campaign culminated in the fall of Kiev, the ancient capital. By now a great deal more was known in western Europe about these strange horsemen from the East, and Matthew of Paris, the chronicler, tells us that they were 'inhuman and beastly, rather monsters than men, thirsting for and drinking blood, tearing and devouring the flesh of dogs and men, dressed in ox-hides, armed with plates of iron, short and stout, thickset, strong, invincible, indefatigable, their backs unprotected, their breasts covered with armour ... they have one-edged swords and daggers, are wonderful archers, spare neither age, nor sex, nor condition.' And, according to Sir John Maudeville, they regarded 'human ears sowced in vynegre' as a particular delicacy.

Kubilai Khan, grandson of Jenghiz, followed up the conquering successes of his family by conquering China, trying unsuccessfully twice to invade Japan, and establishing the Yuan dynasty, which reigned all over China for 100 years. Marco Polo, who stayed at the Khan's court in Pekin from 1275 to 1295, has left a vivid impression of the life of the Tartars, particularly of their battle tactics. 'When they join battle with their enemies these are the tactics by which they prevail. They are never ashamed to have recourse to flight. They manœuvre freely, shooting at the enemy, now from this quarter, now from that. They have trained their horses so well that they wheel this way as quickly as a dog would do. When they are fleeing at top speed, they twist round with their bows and let fly their arrows to such good purpose that they kill the horses of the enemy and the riders too. As soon as the Tartars decide that they have killed enough of the pursuing horses and horsemen, they wheel round and attack and acquit themselves so well and so courageously that they gain a complete victory.'

To quell an uprising which was being mounted against the Great Khan by a rebellious uncle, who, according to Marco, 'raised a force of 400,000 horsemen', Kubilai Khan set out with his army to meet the offender and rode for twenty days until they eventually came to a great plain where the opposition was assembled. Marco Polo then describes the battle that followed: 'When the day of battle dawned, the Great Khan suddenly appeared on a mount that rose from the plain where Nayan's forces were bivouacked.' The enemy were quite at their ease and had no suspicion that they were being caught unawares: 'And suddenly there was the Great Khan on the hill. He stood on the top of a wooden tower, full of crossbowmen and archers, which was carried by four elephants wearing stout leather armour draped with cloths of silk and gold. His troops were marshalled in thirty squadrons of 10,000 mounted archers each, grouped in three divisions,' and in addition there were 15,000 foot soldiers who were so trained that whenever the cavalry decided to retreat, 'they would jump on the horses' cruppers and flee with them.'

'When both parties were lined up in battle array, so that nothing remained but to come to blows, then might be heard a tumult of many instruments, the shrilling of fifes and the sound of men singing at the pitch of their voices.

For the usage of the Tartars is such that when they are confronting the foe and marshalled for the fray they do not join battle till the drums begin to beat—that is the drums of the commander. While they wait for the beat of the drums, all the Tartar host sound their instruments and join in song. That is why the noise of instruments and of singing was so loud on both sides alike.

'When all the troops were in readiness on both sides, then the drums of the Great Khan began to beat. After that there was no more delay; but the two armies fell upon each other with bow and sword and club, and a few with lances. The foot-soldiers had crossbows also and other weapons in plenty. What more shall I say? This was the start of a bitter and bloody battle. Now you might see arrows flying like pelting rain, for the whole air was full of them. Now you might see horsemen and horses tumbling dead upon the ground. So loud was the shouting and the clash of arms that you could not have heard the thunder of heaven.'

The scale of this battle was enormous. According to Marco's report, there must have been a total of about three-quarters of a million soldiers in both armies engaged in one day's fighting, and this was after a travelled distance of five or even seven hundred miles. 'The battle raged from daybreak to noon . . . in the end the victory fell to the Great Khan.' The control of such forces must have presented a mammoth problem, and the marshalling of the Khan's forces operated on an ingenious system that relied on instant obedience to verbal commands. There was one captain in command of every ten soldiers, one of every 100, one of every 1,000 and one of every 10,000, so that the supreme commander never needed to consult with more than ten men. In the same way each commander of 10,000 of 1,000 or 100 consulted only with his ten immediate subordinates, and each man was answerable to his own chief. At each stage the order was promptly received and executed, 'For they are all obedient to the word of command more than any other people in the world,' declared Marco Polo.

There are strange features of the Mongolian story which give it a fantastic, even magic, quality for the romantic, and which constitute puzzles for the historian which can be summed up in three questions. How did a world conqueror suddenly appear within the wilderness, forge great armies out of nothing, and accomplish the overthrow of great cities

A perceptive study by V. M. Vasnetsov of the aftermath of war. Victims of the Battle of Igor Swiatoslaw (972 AD)

72

and civilizations? How did this enormous and well-governed empire come to be so short-lived and collapse so completely? How was it that the Mongols promptly left the world's stage, relapsing into obscurity and stagnation that lasted more than half a millennium? One answer to all three questions could be found in the logistic advantages which gave the Mongols a military superiority over their enemies. Utilizing the skills and organization inherent in nomadism—the swiftness, toughness and lightness of the horsemen, the ability of the tribe in seasonal trek to move, like a military machine, in supple decimals, tens, hundreds, thousands, and tens of thousands—a determined and well-commanded force was able to cover vast distances. The empire extended to half the civilized world, but by the very fact that it was able to spread itself so widely, Mongolia itself was drained of people and thus the empire had no core. The conquests, dramatic as they were at the time, could not be sustained, and the lack of a dynamic and restless leader allowed stagnation to creep in. A conquest of Mongolia would have been a fruitless and wasteful enterprise as there was nothing to conquer. Ivor Montagu, the intrepid traveller, after a visit to Outer Mongolia, declared that 'it was a great empty land like no other in the world, which had

73

seen little change since the time of the great Jenghiz Khan himself—until 1921 when it revolted against Manchu–Chinese suzerainty and declared itself independent.'

The use of the composite bow by the Tartars and the Mongols tends to disprove the literate theory which we mentioned in connection with the Turks. One special fascination of this part of our story are the problems raised in connection with the technical abilities of the nomads of the steppes, and there are numerous unanswered questions as to how the knowledge of bowyery was developed, what systems were employed for the manufacture of countless bows and arrows of a highly specialized nature, and whether or not there were established 'factories' for such production. However, we do know from Marco Polo's stay in Pekin that Kubilai Khan had his palace there and, in addition, there were eight other palaces which served as arsenals each devoted to a particular type of munition. One contained saddles, bridles, stirrups and other items of a horse's harness. In another were bows, bow-strings, quivers, arrows and other requisites of archery, in a third were cuirasses, corselets, and other armours of boiled leather, and so on with the rest. We can therefore conclude that supplies of bows and arrows, among other warlike items, were carefully stored and issued in a regular manner. This leads us to assume that manufacture was probably carried out at either a local centre or at other special places. Marco Polo speaks of Kerman, a kingdom on the edge of Persia, under Tartar rule. 'The inhabitants excel in the manufacture of all equipment of the mounted warrior—bridles, saddles, spurs, swords, bows, quivers, and every sort of armour according to local usage,' and in view of the fact that bow-making in particular was a highly specialized craft, there were probably other similar centres for obtaining supplies.

The characteristic Mongolian bow remained as a standard and recognizable type, and was used in warfare in the hands of Oriental peoples again and again in the centuries that followed the conquests of the Tartars. The persistence with which the bow remained as a weapon of the descendants of the hordes from the steppes is a remarkable feature of its history—Napoleon met with it on his Russian campaign, the Tsar saw it in use by the Tartars in 1900, and the use of archery and horse-riding still persist as national pastimes in the Peoples Republic of Mongolia of today.

CHAPTER 4

Bowmen of the East

The drift of peoples across thousands of miles of the interior wilderness of Asia established new dynasties, replaced older ones, and changed the pattern of history for the area from the Sea of Japan to the Mediterranean. These successive waves of aggression and occupation, more politely described in modern times as colonization, were made possible particularly by the horse and the bow. There were, of course, other weapons, but long-range archery was incontestable compared with hand-to-hand fighting, and with the addition of the mobility of highly trained horses, there was little defence to be had from determined attack from well-organized warrior nomads.

When the Mongols invaded and conquered China in the thirteenth century, the military resistance they met was weak, as the people they subdued had a deep-rooted aversion to things military which was inherent in Chinese civilization. For two millennia or more China had survived as a feudal society with varying periods of peace and strife. During her history there were many wars in China, but these were the result either of the presence of covetous enemies on their borders, such as the Mongols, or of rebellions due to political instability. There is a reluctance on the part of the Chinese people themselves to remember very much of the history of their warfare—not so surprising, when one considers the fact that their great religions are all fundamentally pacific.

However, in China, from the very early times until the end of the eighteenth century, the bow ranked as one of

75

the principal weapons of war, and even until the end of the nineteenth century certain units of the Chinese army retained the bow as an official weapon. The earliest pictures of the bow in China date from the Shang dynasty (about 1500–1028 BC), and although these inscriptions show that the Chinese knew the composite reflex bow at this early stage there is a disappointing lack of further knowledge which would tell us the precise details. Neither do we know to what extent the bow was used in warfare. That it was used as a weapon there can be little doubt; one intriguing theory worthy of consideration points to the fact that powerful bows were associated with nomadic invaders. The ideographs which make up the Chinese character for 'eastern barbarians', when separated, mean 'large' and 'bow'. This is an intriguing blending of meaning, which supports the theory of the bow being used in aggressive situations at an early date in China. Rausing suggests that the composite bow was introduced from the West at an early date, in the early or middle Neolithic. This, he maintains, is indicated

A cavalier of the Lysowski Regiment, superbly equipped for battle, entitled The Polish Rider *by Rembrant van Ryn*

76

by the fact that the composite bow had already found its way to Japan in middle Neolithic times and that it was also widely used in Siberia at the same time. The use of the new weapon could not have spread all the way to Japan without being introduced into northern China.

During the time of the Chou dynasty (1126–256 BC) the composite bow was the most important weapon of the Chinese soldier. Contemporary texts often mention the use of archery in battle. The *Shih King*, for example, mentions an attack on a tribe called the Huai I: 'Behold how they draw their horn bows'—the mention of horn being a reference to the horn component of the composite bow—and another passage seems to refer to a similar aspect of bow construction: 'Two bows strengthened with bone.' Several other passages mention battles in which archery was a decisive factor. We have no precise details of how these battles were conducted, but one unusual feature of early Chinese warfare, which is associated with the Chou dynasty, was based on the existence of a code of military etiquette known as *Li*, which indicates that much so-called war was not serious, but fought for amusement, honour and prestige. Mean tactics, such as attacking the enemy while crossing a river, or picking an opponent much older than oneself, were condemned. A challenge issued to an opposing ruler by a Chou general to do battle, began with the words, 'Will your Excellency permit our knights and yours to play a game?' The actual method of fighting is reminiscent of the heroic age of Greece. The aristocratic champion rode into battle in a four-horse chariot, clad in leather armour and with a powerful bow for a weapon. He was accompanied in the chariot by a driver, and sometimes a lancer also, while a company of foot-soldiers, lightly armed, followed each chariot.

The Chinese bow of the Han dynasty (206 BC–AD 221) cannot be distinguished from that of the nomad peoples, especially from that of the Hiung-Nu, the Hun invaders of central Asia. This dynasty existed during the last part of the 'period of the warring states', during which warfare was in deadly earnest. There was a struggle for power among the greater nobility, and nomadic invasions also had to be repelled. This period saw the growth of the infantry, tough peasants who became exceedingly numerous and of far more tactical significance than components of previous armies. Significant also was the bow and arrow which, together with the javelin and short sword, formed the normal weapons of the Chinese armies. In the same period there was also a development in fortifications and siegecraft, essentially the same as in early European warfare. This era saw the building of the Great Wall, 1,600 miles long and built to repel the invasions by the warlike nomads. The patrolling of this and other frontiers was a major task which continued for centuries. In the T'ang dynasty (AD 618–906), the 'golden age of lyric verse', poems by Lu Lwun describe the lot of the border guards, and in one particular poem an unnamed general is featured issuing new orders to his troops:

> He carried condor fletched arrows called Jin Pu Gu
> And flew an embroidered swallow-tailed pennant named
>   Mau Hu;
> He stood alone and proclaimed the new orders,
> A great cry arose from a thousand camps.

The exact significance of the general's next act is obscure, but it does suggest a symbol of strength and archery skill:

> With darkness emanating from the forests and the wind
>   noisily blowing through the grass,
> The general stepped into the night and drew his bow;
> Came daylight he went afar looking for his arrow,
> And found it with its head buried in a stone.

The T'ang dynasty finally lost power to the Sung as a result of a military coup in the north. In turn this dynasty suffered a setback by the establishment of the Chin Empire in northern China in 1126 by yet another barbarian tribe, the Jurched from Manchuria. In 1280 the Mongol invaders, led by Jenghiz Khan, wiped out the Chin, but it took a further forty-five years to subdue the remainder of China, largely because the horsemen of the steppes were not used to fighting in a populous country with walled cities.

At the beginning of the seventeenth century a race of foreign overlords came out of the northern forests of what is now Manchuria, to fight their way slowly down to Pekin. These Tungus tribes, who abandoned their native forests for the silken cushions of the south, had as their leader Nurhaci, whose military genius had previously been welcomed by the Chinese. During 1592, when the Japanese under the great Hideyoshi invaded Korea, the Koreans

The symbols of power in the Chinese army were bows and arrows ostentatiously displayed as shown in this nineteenth-century engraving of a warrior chieftain

Descendants of the eastern Tartars preserved their ancestral archery traditions until the twentieth century. This early photograph shows the long, stiff 'ears' of the typical Mongol bows which gave additional power and enabled very long arrows to be used, a style which survived in the same form for hundreds of years

appealed to the Chinese for help to repel the invaders. In response to this appeal Nurhaci offered to lead a Tungus battalion against the enemy, but was not called on to fulfil his promise. From 1618 Nurhaci waged war on the Chinese, and this led to the conquest of that empire by the Manchus. In contemporary illustrations he can be seen leading his armies of horse- and foot-archers, who are armed with composite bows and massive quivers full of heavily fletched arrows. In 1644 a Tungus Son of Heaven, the first of ten, was installed in the Forbidden City. These eastern Tartars succeeded in establishing a reigning house of China which lasted until 1912.

The wealth of illustrative material, ranging from primitive rock carvings to early photographic records, shows archers of Asia using composite bows being drawn back in a way different from the Western style, where the archers are using wooden bows. The principal difference is in the 'loose', or method of drawing back and releasing the bowstring. The Western style involves hooking two or three fingers over the string and drawing the arrow back across the left-hand side of the bow. The Asiatic method, where a composite bow is used, involves hooking the thumb, protected by a ring of special design, over the string and locking it in position by folding over it one or more fingers of the same hand. In this case the arrow is drawn back across the right-hand side of the bow. Studies of these release methods

80

have enabled researchers to identify types of bows and even nationalities of the bowmen. The protective rings vary in design according to the country of origin and this is another factor that enables material relics to be more precisely identified. The general design of these thumb-rings from China is a rather bulky cylinder of semi-precious stone such as jade or agate; from India and Turkey the form is a slimmer, spade-shaped ring usually of ivory, and in Japan this method of release was adopted during the period of the Mongol rule in China (1279–1368), encouraging the development of a unique stiffened glove, which embodied the essential features of the Asiatic release technique.

The technical aspects of these different release methods have been subjects of absorbing interest for students of ballistics and bow performance. The characteristics of the bows themselves have broadly dictated the method of release. For example, the composite bow is capable of being bent farther than a wooden bow and, accordingly, a longer arrow can be used, with consequential increase of power. It is physically more awkward to draw back a bow-string beyond the centre of the body with the fingers hooked over the string, but with the thumb-hook it becomes easier. Another aspect was the technique of release developed by horse-archers. This consisted of twisting the bow outwards at the moment of release to obtain extra momentum to the arrow. If the arrow was on the left side of the bow, assuming that the bow was held in the left hand, this action would not be possible, and a release by means of fingers does not work unless the arrow is on the left. The thumb-hook works perfectly if the arrow is shot from the right of the bow. There are numerous complex technicalities relating to bow-release, in addition to all the other specialized aspects of archery; several thousand years ago these matters were resolved, either by accident or design, and the principles have not changed since, nor can they be improved upon.

The form of archery that blossomed in Japan, and which is principally associated with the samurai, was unique. Popular notions of the part they played in the history of Japan are often restricted to an impression of a body of charging, screaming warriors on horseback, discharging battle-shafts with wild abandon at all and sundry. Whereas the samurai were essentially mounted archers, the story of their warlike occupation cannot be fully understood unless

*A samurai warrior in
full battle panoply.
The two* Wuwagashi
*(upper arrows),
reserved for shooting
high-ranking warriors,
are shown segregated
from the remainder in
the quiver*

one has regard to the medieval feudal system of knighthood, which involved deeds of incredible ferocity and an almost morbid sense of personal honour. Coupled with this was a sense of the symbolic as well as the physical power of the bow, and a unique system of training in its use.

The history of Japan, and of its archery, is inextricably linked with legends and tradition, and fact and fiction are often so intermingled that it is practically impossible to divorce one from the other. But the familiar story of invasion and domination, the establishment of a new nation and the driving out of the old began with the last descendants of a dying race, the Ainu, living on Sakhalin, the large island at the northern extremity of Japan. During the Neolithic period, somewhere between 3000–1800 BC, these people were already resident in Japan, and from a thorough study of bones and fossils taken from Neolithic graves it is apparent that this ancient stock had spread its culture over the whole archipelago before another race started to overrun the country. Sea-borne raids and invasion by the adventurous forebears of the Japanese were resisted time and time again by the Ainu, who were, to say the least, indignant that the safety of their homeland was threatened. Indignity and threats became humiliation and defeat, and eventually the Ainu were driven north and south. Ultimately those in the south were decimated; a remnant of these Indo-Europeans were left on Hokkaido and Sakhalin in the north. From that time they decreased in number, until today they are a tourist attraction exhibited as an ethnological miracle.

The ancient histories of Japan refer again and again to skirmishes with the Ainu, whose brave but ineffectual resistance continued for many hundreds of years. Undoubtedly the invaders' weapons were far superior to the primitive equipment used by the original inhabitants, for whereas the latter were using stone points for their arrows the former employed well-made arrow-heads of bronze and later of iron. One of the finds among the Neolithic shell-mounds of Kyushu, the southernmost of the four major islands of the Japanese group, was an iron arrow-head under the rib-bones of one of the skeletons buried there. Its shape is approximately the same as others found in the proto-historic dolmens of Japan, and indicates a high degree of manufacturing skill in addition to a knowledge of the requirements of a specialized missile point. An early chronicle of Japan, dated AD 720, is said to mention bows, spears and swords in a legendary account of a migratory invasion by Japanese tribesmen—more than a thousand years earlier—of an island now thought to be Kyushu, and it is generally accepted that it was on this island that the earliest ancestral Japanese settled. The mute testimonies of bone and iron help to confirm the legendary histories of unsuccessful resistance by the Ainu. The methods of warfare can be imagined—a determined, well-organized, barbaric invasion force, equipped with superior arms, taking by surprise a settlement of peaceable and bewildered aborigines whose archery was used more for hunting than for war.

But it was the invaders who came across the sea to take the whole of Japan who were the ancestors of a remarkable nation now totalling over one hundred million souls. Wherever they came from, they brought with them basic skills from which were developed incredible techniques of manufacture and artistry. After much tribal strife a group known as the Yamato emerged during the first three or four centuries of the Christian era, whose leaders are generally accepted as the ancestors of the present Imperial family. Through Korea, industrial arts such as weaving, metal-work, tanning and shipbuilding were introduced into Japan. Later the Chinese script was adopted, and in 538 Buddhism was brought to Japan from India by way of China and Korea. It is not unlikely that both the bows and the technique of Japanese use are of north-east Asian origin. One fact that points in this direction is that among certain proto-historic remains in Japan there have been found a number of turnip-shaped sound-making arrow-heads almost identical in design to similar arrow-heads common in Mongolia and formerly peculiar to the Mongolians. On the other hand, there is no evidence to support any contention that the Japanese bow is of southern origin. The Malayans did not use the bow at all, and in Formosa the present wild tribes used a very primitive weapon, probably based on the bow used in China and Indo-China.

Curiously shaped and bearing little resemblance to any other bow the world over, the weapon used by the Japanese has not altered in design for over 1,000 years. Its shape is not symmetrical, the arc being somewhat flatter at one end, and usually there are marked recurves—that is to say the

A victim's eye-view of a Japanese warrior taking aim at close range. The bow has been shortened by the artist, which increases the dramatic effect of pent-up energy about to be released

tips curve slightly in the opposite direction to the main sweep. This recurving is more pronounced when the bow is unstrung. The most unusual feature, and one which is completely alien to good principles of bowyery, is the location of the handle or grip. This is positioned some two-thirds of the way down the bow instead of in the conventional mid-way position which is normal practice. This makes the limbs of unequal length, an unsatisfactory and unstable arrangement.

From a number of bows belonging to famous warriors of the past and preserved in various temples and shrines, it is apparent that the average length of a traditional Japanese bow has not altered for at least six or seven hundred years. There are some very long specimens, which are the exception rather than the rule, such as the one belonging to Yuasa Matashi-chiro which is eight feet nine inches long, and another, four inches shorter, which was used by Ihara Koshiro. Several bows preserved at the temple of Mishima average about seven feet seven inches, one of which was dedicated to the temple in 1363, while that which belonged to the famous Minamoto Yoritomo,

An incident in the feuding battles between rival Japanese families for power in the twelfth century. The central figure is Sasaki Takatsuma, facing a shower of arrows from troops under Yoshitsune in the Uji river. From a kakemono *of about 1890*

86

in the temple of Hachimangu at Tsurugaoka, measured only six feet five inches. These bows must have been very powerful, and render less improbable the story that it took three ordinary men to bend the bow of Tametomo, which was eight feet six inches long. Minamoto Tametomo was very tall, his arms being so abnormally long that he could, it was reported, draw a bowstring eighteen hands-breadths—about five feet.

The construction and style of the bows used by the ancient Japanese prior to the dating of the specimens preserved in temples are not definitely known. It is probable that the pattern did not vary much from that which has been described, although the construction may have been from a single stave of wood. There is also no certainty that the development of these singular bows took place before or after the Japanese conquered their new homeland, and many theories have been advanced to account for the evolution of their asymmetrical shape. The contention that they were designed so as to easily be manageable on horseback is arguable. That the short stature of the Japanese demanded a bow that would clear the ground when held perpendicularly is not acceptable, because if the handle were set halfway down the bow it would still give ample clearance. The kneeling position of shooting which was practised by armoured warriors, does call for a shorter lower limb to the bow, and this could conceivably be a factor that encouraged this practice of construction. An explanation involving the development of this weapon from the primitive sapling which, tapering as it did, needed a grip some two-thirds of the way down to effect some sort of dynamic balance, is intriguing and worthy of study. Among the treasures of the Imperial Shosoin, in Nara, there are preserved specimens of ancient bows made from a single stem of *azusa* (catalpa), the lower third of which has been somewhat worked down to increase the flexibility of the butt end of the stem. Later specimens show an improvement in design where two stems were used, spliced together, thus avoiding the necessity of working down the lower limb. Here was a chance to regularize the position of the grip, but even at that early date tradition was at work, and tradition called for a bow grip to be where it had always been. This would seem to be the simplest and possibly the most likely explanation for the unique form of the Japanese bow.

This was the mighty bow immortalized in the ancient chronicles of Japan. In their ceaseless pursuit of chivalric warfare the samurai performed many deeds in battle which not only brought out the best qualities of personal honour and bravery, involving astounding acts of devotion and self-sacrifice, but also amply displayed an unrivalled prowess with the bow. Many of these exploits are fantastic by our standards, and belief in them requires a feeling for the legendary aspect of history. An elaborate ceremonial code involving the bow and arrow is closely associated with the rise of Japanese military domination.

The first permanent capital of Japan was established in Nara at the beginning of the eighth century, and for the following seventy-four years emperors reigned from there with a growing authority over the country. In 784, however, a new capital was established in Kyoto, modelled after the Chinese capital of those days, and the Heian period occupied the next four centuries, until 1192. Japan's contacts with China were interrupted at the close of the ninth century, and subsequently her civilization began to assume its own particular form and characteristics. In some ways the Heian period was an age of elegance; the example was set by the highest in the land, and soon it became fashionable to indulge in the arts and sports of the nobility.

As court officials whiled away the time with elegant banquets and games, local clans gradually came into power on the strength of their armed forces. They ignored the orders of the central government, and low-ranking military clans in government service began to gain influence. There were two important military families, the Minamotos and the Tairas, descendants of separate emperors, and after a series of internecine struggles for power the Minamotos annihilated the Tairas in 1185. The legendary histories of these battles are full of incidents involving archery and, according to these reports, the Japanese warrior was no mean shot. He was also superbly equipped and a fearsome sight in full battle array, positively bristling with swords, spears, bows and quivers full of arrows, and dressed in a complicated armour of lacquer plates held together by silken cords, embellished with elaborate ornament. All this was worn with a studied correctness. However, the final ostentatious blossoming of the Japanese medieval knight in his full panoply was to come later.

In 1192 Yorimoto, head of the Minamoto family, established the Shogunate (military camp government) at Kamakura, thus marking the beginning of 600 years of feudal government. The new régime remained in power until 1338, and this reign is known as the Kamakura period. During these years emphasis was placed on stabilizing the country by strengthening the ties of loyalty between the Shogun and his vassals. At the same time they tried to prepare for emergencies by encouraging chivalry.

By 1259 Kubilai Khan had become emperor of China and he moved his capital to Pekin in 1264. By this time Korea had acknowledged the supremacy of the Mongols, and, as Stephen Turnbull reminds us in his book *Samurai*, Mongol power stretched to within fifty miles of Japanese territory. Diplomatic moves were instigated with Japan which amounted to a threat of war unless Japan acknowledged Mongol supremacy. The representation from Kubilai in-

A late thirteenth-century illustration of a samurai warrior in full battle regalia during the Mongol invasions

cluded a phrase which, in translation, has a very familiar ring. 'When we first ascended the throne, many innocent people in Korea were suffering from continuous war. Thereupon we put an end to the fighting, restored their territories, and liberated the captives both young and old.' The belief by megalomaniacs throughout history that invasion and subjugation should properly be described as 'liberation' is nothing new, and the Japanese, recognizing the thinly veiled intimation, began hasty preparations to defend their kingdom.

The fleet that carried the first Mongol invasion army of some 25,000 troops set sail in November 1274, and after capturing the islands of Tsushima and Iki, they met fierce Japanese resistance. However, the Japanese skill in combat was single, hand-to-hand fighting, and they were no match for a massed army, trained in close formation manœuvring, with a lifetime of battle experience. The situation was saved by a severe storm, and the Mongol generals were persuaded to re-embark and return to Korea to avoid the risk of becoming isolated on shore. A second invasion was planned, and the ensuing seven years saw the assembling of what turned out to be the greatest overseas expeditionary force the world had yet seen, and the complete mobilization of the resources of Japan's manpower and wealth for defence. In 1281 the second invasion began and the clash of these two powers continued for seven weeks. Then the weather intervened again and a violent hurricane blew up and raged for two days. When it subsided the Great Khan's armada had been battered into uselessness. At least half the Mongol force of 100,000 had been drowned or cut down when they tried to re-embark. The hurricane became known as the *kami-kaze*, or 'divine wind', literally regarded as a weapon from heaven, which came to be seen as a symbol of Japan's divine protection. The suicide pilots of the Second World War adopted the name *kami-kaze*, deliberately identifying themselves with the divine tempest.

To support a claim for compensation and reward, one of the warriors who served the national cause commissioned the *Mongol Invasion Scroll* in 1293, which includes a multitude of wonderful details of both the Mongol and Japanese armies. For example, we can observe individual bowmen in action, their equipment clearly shown, and we can study the significant differences between, for instance, the shorter

In the height of battle; attackers returning the Japanese defenders' arrow-shot during the Mongol invasions of 1274–81

composite bows of the Mongols and the longer and slimmer Japanese laminated weapons. The Mongol arrows are shorter than the Japanese, with smaller fletchings, and they are carried in hip quivers, often with flaps to protect them when travelling, whereas the Japanese arrows are carried in shoulder quivers in great fan-like displays of feathers. The Japanese have far more elaborate and complicated armour and we can even detect the *tsurumaki*, a wicker reel for carrying spare bow-strings, hanging from the warriors' belts—still a standard item in the kit of archers in Japan.

The samurai, whose code of chivalry became known as *bushido*, recognized warfare as a special art. Individual accuracy rather than massed flight was the accepted use of archery in battle, and all training and practice was directed with this in mind. These select and highly respected (and feared) warriors first appeared in the twelfth century, and an author of a slightly later date speaks thus of them and their ways: 'Their ponderous bows are *San-nin-bari* (a bow needing three ordinary men to bend it) or *Go-nin-bari* (five-

91

men bows); their quivers, which match their bows, hold fourteen or fifteen bundles of arrows. They are very quick in their release, and each arrow kills or wounds two or three foemen, the impact being powerful enough to pierce two or three thicknesses of armour at a time: and they never fail to hit the mark. Every *Daimyo* (owner of a great estate) has at least twenty or thirty of such mounted archers, and even the owner of a small barren estate has two or three. It is the habit of the *Kwanto-Bushi* that if in the field of battle a father falls, the son will not retreat, or if a son be slain, the father will not yield, but stopping over the dead they will fight to the death.'

Further insight into the high ideals of courage and personal valour of the samurai is illustrated by an episode in the protracted siege of Kanazawa. In the camp of Yoshiiye, who strove to imbue his troops with a sense of discipline and a proper respect for military virtues, orders were issued for a singularly unusual arrangement. Special seats were set apart for the brave and for the shirkers, and after each assault the warriors were assigned to their places according to their deserts. A youth of sixteen, a certain Kamakura Gongoro, a Taira by birth, received an arrow in the eye in the course of one of the assaults. He merely snapped off the shaft, and then returned his enemy's fire and brought down the man who had hit him. When he took off his helmet he tumbled to earth with the barb still in his eye; and when a friend, in extracting it, put his foot on his face to give himself a purchase, the youthful warrior swore he would have his life for subjecting him to such an indignity, for to trample on the face of a *Bushi* was an outrage that could only be expiated by the blood of the offender.

The military spirit of the Kamakura period was in complete contrast to the fastidious taste of Heian times and, although it originated far earlier, it was under Minamoto no Yoritomo (1145–95) that *bushido* took on its own permanent form. Moreover Zen Buddhism now gave it its metaphysical and religious bases, and it became a philosophy of death practised in life. The principle of the Japanese knightly ethic is represented by the bow and the sword, symbols of inner purity, for the samurai perfected a technique for transcending death in the hour of death, by regarding it objectively. This was the art of enlightenment for the warrior; by making no distinction between life and death *bushido* eliminated the gap between them.

The importance of dying an honourable death preoccupied the minds of these philosophic warriors, and sooner than die in dishonour they preferred to die of their own free will. Death on the battlefield was natural and inevitable but must needs be honourable, and this tenet was interpreted in many ways which to Western minds have a curious and unfathomable quality. For instance, an arrow intended to be used against a general had to be of superior and more elaborate design than that shot at a private. This was taken to extreme lengths by the provision of two special arrows, known as *Wuwagashi* (upper arrows), in a standard set of twenty-four. These were reserved for shooting high-ranking warriors, and if such an officer was killed by a bow-shot intended for a lesser rank his fate was regarded as death by a stray arrow.

At the beginning of the fourteenth century the warrior Kamakura government was overthrown, and a breakaway group set up a rival emperor. The conflict between the two emperors of Japan and their courts, and disputes over succession, threw the country into fifty years of civil war. The warrior chiefs continued to rule their own domains and each man became his own defender. High constables and land stewards became feudal lords, making their own laws and raising their own armies. Fighting between rival clans and power factions continued for another 200 years, with the samurai always in the forefront of battle armed with the mighty bow. The history of this period is scattered with near-legendary feats of the warlords, the heroes of this unique period, and numerous examples of incredible feats of archery in battle can be cited to illustrate the borderline between fantasy and reality.

Without doubt the samurai were highly trained bowmen and possessed skills that were performed largely to proclaim their own personal achievement and prowess. For example, Tametomo, a descendant of Minamoto Yoshiiye, the first Japanese archer of renown, distinguished himself in the first battle between the Taira and Minamoto clans in 1156. 'The action began with the shouting of war cries, pedigrees and personal achievements. There followed an archery duel in the dark, during which Tametomo caused great alarm by sending an arrow clean through one samurai to wound another . . . he loosed another arrow at Yoshimoto's helmet.

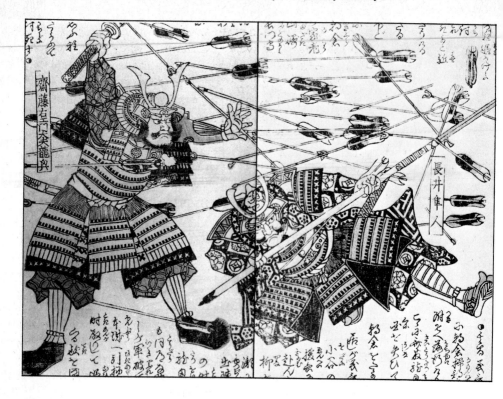

The arrow tore off one of the projecting rivets and buried itself in the gatepost. Tametomo was about to loose another shaft when he was challenged by two samurai who addressed him as follows:

> We are descendants of Kamakura Gongoro who, when he was sixteen years old in the Three Years' War of Hachiman Taro, went out in the van of battle and was hit in the left eye by an arrow....'

Then followed an account of the incident which occurred at the siege of Kanazawa. Any descendant of Kamakura Gongoro was a worthy opponent for Tametomo: '... he fixed a "humming bulb" arrow to his bow and let fly. The arrow made a loud scream as it flew through the air, and cut off at the knee the left leg of Oba Kageyoshi, who was standing about twenty yards away, the arrow passed on and hit his horse....'

About the middle of the sixteenth century the bow was ousted by the arquebus, and by 1600 it was considered old fashioned, although some diehards insisted on carrying it into battle. The samurai were abolished as a class in 1860,

Samurai warriors locked in mortal combat in the classic form of individual contest. Note the different forms of arrow-heads

94

having since the turn of the seventeenth century been 'essentially an unproductive bunch of under-employed parasites'. This revelation is curiously coincidental, as the peak of samurai militarism, prior to 1615, were those centuries when the bow and arrow were considered supreme. It is tempting to suggest that the substitution of firearms for the bow not only removed from the arena of contest the ancient and traditional weapon itself, but also removed a special symbolism relating to warlike motivation, the absence of which allowed knightly tempers to cool and Oriental chivalry to founder.

The great sub-continent of India, inhabited in historical times by peoples of at least eight distinct races professing many different faiths and speaking some 200 different languages and dialects, presents such a kaleidoscope of contrasts that it is well-nigh impossible to deal with its archery other than in a general fashion. From the fourth millennium BC until the nineteenth century AD the bow was the chief weapon in India. Because of the time factor, the overlapping in racial origins, and the variety of technological innovation, there are a range of bow types ranging from the most primitive to the most sophisticated.

Some aspects of the Indian civilization stretch back for more than 4,000 years, during which time countless invasions of that country took place. The great majority of India's invaders came through the passes of the north-west, from Persia or central Asia. The armies of Cyrus and Darius of Persia passed this way; so did the forces of Alexander the Great, of the Bactrian Greeks, the Kushans and the Huns. From AD 700 there began a series of Muslim invasions, the last and most important being the coming of the Mughals—a corruption of Mongols—in the sixteenth century.

The composite bow was first introduced to India by the wandering tribes from the Near East who settled in the Indus valley, which offers an environment not unlike that of Babylonia; in fact, the civilization which developed there clearly appears to be related to that of the latter, and there was certainly trade between the two regions. Luristan, primarily the area of the Zagros Mountains which provide the western physical boundary of Persia, is particularly rich in archaeological finds of fine-quality bronze arrow-heads, and the early progress of the composite bow can be conjectured from the similarity of these early finds, in pattern and age, to those associated with the early types of Assyrian and Mesopotamian bows. The sites of the early Indian civilizations stretched along some 800 miles of the coast from the modern Persian frontier, and inland from the south of the Indus, through Sind and Punjab to the foothills of the Himalayas. It seems that a series of city states was formed in the Indus valley, and the absence there of advanced weapons of bronze or copper suggests the security of these cities and the absence of aggressors; but this military unpreparedness made them an easy prey to invasion when it came. The first major irruption was made by the warlike Aryan tribes, bringing horses and chariots and the composite bow from Iran.

There is a similarity in the ancient literature of India to that of Japan, in that it is often difficult to sift the fact from the fiction. However, to have written about a bow, even in a far-fetched manner, means that at least the weapon was a familiar object, and it is probable that accounts of it were based on fact.

As early as 1,000 years or more before Christ the oral traditions of the Vedic period were being recorded, and in the famous battle-hymn in the *Rig Veda* the bow and arrow are the most applauded of all the weapons mentioned. The warrior is described in his chariot armed with bow and arrow and dressed in armour, wearing a guard to protect his arm from the friction of the bow-string. The bow was the best loved of a warrior's possessions. It was removed from the right hand of a dead man in the last act of the funeral rite. In other Vedic literature there are descriptions of the stringing of the bow ready for use, the placing of the arrow, the bending of the bow and the shooting of the shaft. Even the method of drawing the string back to the ear and the sound of the twang of the bow-string were meticulously, even romantically described.

> Close to his ear as fain to speak, she presses, holding her well-loved friend in her embraces
> Strained on the bow she whispers like a woman, this bow-string that preserves us in combat.

The military tradition was continued in the Epic literature around 600 to 400 BC and, as in the earlier period, the bow and arrow is the supreme weapon. It is likely that there

96

was a 'heroic' period in Indian warfare, similar to the Greek and Chinese warfare, when battles were multiple duels between aristocratic charioteers accompanied by retainers on foot. Every knight of note was a distinguished archer, and the best bowmen invariably decided the fate of an armed engagement. A variety of arrows was used, most being made of reed or cane with many different and sometimes curious forms of arrow-heads. For example, some which were knife-shaped were said to be capable of severing a head from the body; another favourite shape was crescent headed, yet another was the shape of a calf's tooth, exceedingly sharp, and there was a broad chisel-ended head, useful for cutting bow-strings, bows and even limbs.

The battles described in the Epics are exaggerated in the familiar way that most legends are, but the original experience must have created a basic pattern that became the truth on which fantasy hung. They should be judged from the practical point of view and toxophilitic evidence should not be lightly dismissed as impossible. Take, for example, the incredible accuracy of the near super-human Epic heroes; the shooting of seven arrows into a barking dog's mouth before he can shut it; or the twenty-one arrows that were shot into a hollow horn swinging on a rope. These and other activities could well have had some basis in the actual human skill of the warrior of the period, a tradition kept alive until at least the opening years of the present century by an Indian archer named Kaliyugi Arjuna. According to an eye-witness account this expert could shoot four arrows simultaneously from the same bow and hit four different targets all at once. He could easily support a football in mid-air for more than five minutes with a continuous shower of arrows. And perhaps the most incredible of feats: 'He smeared sharp arrow-tips with chalk dust and shot them at the bare backs of students with a perfect delicacy of control, so that they left only chalk marks on their tender targets without even grazing them.'

The scenes of battle in the Epics describe networks of arrows crossing and cutting one another in mid-air. Bows are rent asunder and bow-strings are cut in two—the archer strikes wherever he likes with an impeccable accuracy of aim. An arrow is often enough to fell even an elephant. Mounted archers, bowmen in chariots and riding on top of elephants, provided the familiar combination of

mobility and fire-power, and these, together with infantry armed with bows and close-range weapons, provided the armies of ancient India.

In 326 BC Alexander the Great invaded India in the north-west and within 100 years or so a further series of invasions brought Bactrian Greeks, Sakas and other peoples of Iranian or central Asian origin into India, where they established kingdoms and were assimilated by the existing population. At the time of Alexander's invasion Indian bows were described by Arrian as follows: 'The Indian infantry have a bow equal in length to the man who carries it. Placing this down to the ground and stepping against it with the left foot, they discharge the arrow, drawing the string far back. Their arrows are little less than three cubits long, and nothing can withstand one shot by an Indian archer, neither shield nor breastplate.'

Arrian may have been too careless an observer or his account may have been shortened, because the method of shooting described by him is hardly practical. The first part more likely describes the stringing of the bow, which is a separate operation from that of shooting it. Also his reported length of an arrow, if the cubit is taken to be about

The short powerful composite bows of the Mughal warriors in this scene of about 1600 AD have inflicted considerable damage on the enemy. Of particular interest is the wounded elephant in the centre of the picture

98

eighteen inches, is surprisingly long compared with most specimens, which are in the order of twenty-eight to thirty inches. The earliest bows in India were made of wood, often bamboo, which was readily obtainable and reasonably strong and flexible. Later the composite bow was introduced by invaders in a long series of incursions by archer-peoples. The two main types evolving were those from the north and south, which vary only slightly, and the Sind bow, the so-called 'crab' bow, which has a marked depression in the handle portion. Essentially the form of Indian composite bow remained exactly the same to that used farther west.

The Hindus never developed mounted archery and the whole concept of Indian warfare progressed little from the elementary tactics of hand-to-hand fighting. The martial

Great fighting towers were erected on the backs of elephants to provide mobile firing platforms high above the enemy

qualities of the Turko-Islamic invaders consistently overcame the Hindus in a long eight centuries of invasion and conquest. Sultan Mahmud of Ghazni led seventeen successful campaigns in India, Timur the Mongol swept through Hindustan in five months and Babur the Tiger, through whose conquests the Moghul Empire was formed, was invincible. These and many other powerful leaders, with their

Although both attackers and defenders in this Indian siege scene are using similar composite bows, the mobility provided by the horses countered the static defensive advantages of height

precisely ordered military organizations and with the skilful use of well-drilled mobile bowmen armed with the inevitably superior composite bow, were victorious over their lesser-skilled opponents.

Despite the deep traditions which have become associated with the Indian use of archery, and all the skills which were developed in bowyery in that country, from the military point of view there are no outstanding innovations in the way the bow was used. The applications of archery in war and the equipment used were all inherited from the many different peoples that successively settled in India. However, these artefacts, which came to be called Indian, were principally altered from an aesthetic rather than a technological aspect, and by their decorative appearance have attracted more attention as works of art rather than tools of war.

CHAPTER 5

Bowmen of Europe

The history of the traditional longbow is often confined to the fourteenth and fifteenth centuries, by which time it had become recognized by military commanders as an important supporting arm. Its superiority as a weapon remained unchallenged through the many classic battles of the Hundred Years War. This was the weapon of the simple man, the yeoman, the Tommy Atkins of the Middle Ages, who, by wielding his bow of yew and clothyard shafts gained a totally unexpected immortality, unique in the annals of medieval warfare, for at that time the lot of the common soldier was to struggle and suffer in complete obscurity. However, the evolutionary background of this great weapon reached back beyond the days of the yeoman, beyond the Norman conquest of Britain, to the days before the Dark Ages descended upon Europe. From the fragmentary evidence that is available it is possible to trace the warlike course of this significant weapon in the form in which it became so familiar. Among the deep-rooted traditions that had originated in Scandinavia were many legends involving the bow, and together with various discoveries of miraculously preserved bows scattered over north-western Europe, they serve to indicate the continuity of the use of that weapon during the restless years which saw many familiar groups of settlers establishing themselves in Britain and Europe.

During the period that followed the withdrawal of the Roman legions from Britain there are accounts of piratical raids by the Saxons, prior to their serious landtakings and

101

before they established wide settlement in England stretching from the Thames to the Tees. Thomas Elyot wrote '...
when the Saxons came first into this realm in King Vor-
tigen's days, when they had been here a while, and at last
began to fall out with the Britons, they troubled and
subdued the Britons with nothing as much as with their bow
and shaft, which weapon being strange, and not seen here
before, was wonderful terrible to them.' Following the Neolithic period there had seemed to be a decline in the use of
the bow, but the Saxon incursions appeared to have reintro-
duced the weapon into England.

A series of splendid longbows emerged from the three
ancient and well-preserved Saxon galleys found in Nydam
Moor in Denmark in 1863. Many of these were made of
yew and they measured between five feet seven inches and
six feet in length. Several other bows, similar to the Nydam
finds, were discovered at Vomose in Schleswig-Holstein. All
these bows have been scientifically dated to between AD 200
and 400, and all closely parallel authentic specimens of military bowstaves salvaged from the wreck of the *Mary Rose*,
which sank in 1545. Another series of important finds which
provides further evidence for the growing use of the longbow in Europe are the bows of yew found in a group of
graves of AD 600 in Oberfracht, near the source of the
Danube.

The Viking era in Britain began at the end of the eighth
century, and their barbarous raids spread over these islands
from Canterbury to York, the Isle of Wight to Ireland, and
from South Wales to Northumbria. They too established
settlements and kingdoms in Britain, and the Norse customs of war and attitudes to the bow must have had some
effect through these periods of cultural imposition and
exchange. These traditions were to be seen in full and at
first hand when the great invasion of Britain brought an
army from the Viking settlement in Normandy under
William the Bastard. The tactics used by the Norsemen were
similar to those practised by the Huns and Tartars,
although the means they employed were different. Their
skills of seamanship provided the basic mobility re-
quirement and the use of the axe and shield were their principal armaments for the surprise lightning attack, rape and
pillage, sack and burn, and equally rapid departure. The
tenth-century bow found on the floor of an Irish crannogh

in Ballinderry, County Meath, of traditional longbow pattern, probably originated in Denmark, as the site at Ballinderry has been established as a Viking settlement.

A special Viking connection with archery is kept alive by the legend of the martyrdom of St. Edmund, who was shot by Danish invaders in 870.

> The cursid Danys of new cruelte
> This martyr took, most gracious and benigne
> Of hasty rancour bounde him to a tree.
> As for their marke to sheete at, and ther signe
> And in this wise, ageyne hym thei maligne,
> Made with him arwis of ther malis most wikke
> Rassemble an Yrchoun fulfilled with spynys thikke.

The fate of Edmund stuck with arrows 'resembling a hedgehog [Yrchoun] full of thick spines' is reminiscent of the similar treatment given to Ursula by the Huns, and to Sebastian by the Romans—all martyred by the bow and all kept alive in the calendar of saints as grim reminders of the 'winged and silent messenger of death'. The modern parallel is the use of a regulation army issue rifle to carry out a death penalty by firing squad, the unfortunate victim, through his transgressions, becoming 'enemy', and his demise perfectly 'legal', as his execution is carried out with an 'official' weapon of war, which, in a curious form of ritualistic symbolism, makes the killing amoral and the killers beyond censure.

The events that led up to the Battle of Hastings have been dealt with by a multitude of historians, and the detailed progress of the battle on Saturday 14 October, 1066, has been set down over and over again, with variations, in a long series of chronicles, accounts and historical studies which begins with the earliest known description of the event, a narrative poem by Guy of Amiens written within two years of the battle. It was not until sixty and more years later that other accounts of that fatal day began to appear, and from all these reports, plus the exciting visual evidence provided by the Bayeux Tapestry, we can reconstruct the whole pattern of what took place and, most importantly for us, the particular part in the battle played by the bow-weapon.

The final outcome of the Battle of Hastings is known by every schoolboy, but the question that has often been posed is: 'What circumstances contributed to King Harold's defeat

103

VM:

CO

Norman archers from the Bayeux Tapestry. They are drawing their arrows to the breast in order to reach the maximum range. In this sequence the archers are supporting the charging Norman cavalry

when every advantage should have been his?' Before we tell the story of the battle let us summarize these advantages. The historic background that led up to this conflict concerned the two boldest warriors of that age, both claiming the right to the throne—although Harold had perjured himself after swearing an oath that he would accept William as king of England after the death of Edward—and both were experienced soldiers who had fought together as brothers-in-arms. Harold, who was some seven or eight years older than William, is supposed to have promised to marry one of William's daughters, and to have taken part with William in a military expedition against the Bretons. They were virtually allies and were clearly aware of each other's potential in battle.

At Stamford Bridge, only three weeks previously, Harold had fought off the threat of Viking invasion, and although the ancient sagas mention the use of bows and arrows on this occasion there is little evidence that the archery talents of the Saxons were properly mobilized. This is curious, for Harold must have experienced the advantages of properly organized archers in the French campaigns, and in fact Duke William of Normandy gave considerable attention to army reorganization, reform, and rearmament in the years 1055 to 1058.

The threat in the north from the invading Norwegian army under Harald Hardraada, king of Norway, was the culmination of several weeks of ravaging the Shetlands and the Orkneys, the Cleveland coast, on to the river Humber and the Yorkshire Ouse, until York itself was in deadly and most imminent peril. In four more days York was invested, Northumbria accepted Harald Hardraada as its king, and the Northumbrians agreed to march southwards with his army. Faced with this threat King Harold of the Saxons had no option but to hasten north to repel the invaders. The outcome was that the Norwegian army was annihilated, 'the English rode upon them from all sides and threw spears and shot at them'. Significantly, the Norse king fell, with an arrow through his throat. Harold Godwinson had at least used archery successfully at this, his finest victory, but the English losses must have been extreme, and his army had been weakened. His success at Stamford Bridge, which has been described as 'one of the most complete victories of the Middle Ages', was to cost King Harold dear.

Three days later William, Duke of Normandy, landed at Pevensey Bay, completing a channel crossing described as 'one of the most important amphibious operations in the history of war'. England's southern shore had been guarded by a few local levies, but they had gone home a couple of weeks previously through lack of supplies and because of the pressing need to gather in the harvest. Without any resistance William was able to establish his base, and the news that England was again threatened by invaders was brought to Harold, probably still in York. He set out to march back to London with all haste, leaving much of his infantry and most of his archers behind. On his southward journey the men of the shires flocked to his banner. He spent a few days in London assembling more troops and then marched south to take up a carefully chosen defensive position seven miles from William's camp, on a spur 'the spot which used to be called Senlac in ancient times' and is now the site of Battle Abbey and the town of Battle.

'Enormous forces of Englishmen had come together from all parts of the country,' and the English army 'had a great numerical advantage', wrote the Norman chroniclers. However, carefully considered research puts the English forces at about 7,000 and the Normans at 1,000 or so less. All on foot, in dense formation with the king and his picked household troops at the centre, the Saxons ranged along the brow of the hill, carrying 'javelins and missiles of all sorts, axes, and stones hafted on to wooden handles'. Some carried swords and those who had armour wore helmets and mail hauberks. Two components were notably absent— horses and archery—both having been used at Stamford Bridge, and this omission was to prove fatal. The Saxon strategy was simple: to hold the line against every attack, defence without any provision for offence. The reason for this is another major question which remains unanswered, particularly as Harold knew only too well how William would be equipped and the strategy he would adopt.

These matters did not escape the notice of the Normans, which must have given them great encouragement; in particular the absence of archers in Harold's army was mentioned by Henry of Huntingdon, who, in his account of the campaign written in the early 1120s, had Duke William mentioning in his speech before the battle 'this people [Saxons] which has come here without even a quiver-ful of arrows'. The great panorama of warriors depicted in the Bayeux Tapestry includes one lone and rather puny Saxon archer, without protection from armour, no quiver-ful of arrows, and shown significantly half the size of his fellow defenders.

'Good pay and broad lands to everyone who will serve Duke William with spear, sword and bow,' was the word in Normandy, and there is every reason to believe that William himself, like so many other distinguished commanders, was a skilled archer. 'None but the Duke William could bend Duke William's bow,' was the proud boast of his minstrels. To be of value a large body of archers had to be kept in constant training and practice, and it appears likely that such a body of troops was held constantly mobilized by the Duke. It is no wonder that on that fateful Saturday in October 1066, the invaders from Normandy—many descended from Viking settlers, a large proportion consisting of battle-hardened troops trained in archery, all well equipped and all well paid and eager to gain 'broad lands'—were able to outmanœuvre the Saxons.

The Norman army made their way across the open countryside until they reached the foot of the hill on which Harold's whole army was massed. The Normans themselves made up the centre of their army, which was disposed in three lines; the bowmen stood in front, next came the infantry, armed, some with bows and arrows, others with javelins, and finally drawn up behind were the squadrons of cavalry, with William himself in their midst. The left and right wings, made up of Bretons and Franco-Flemish mercenaries, were similarly arrayed.

A lone and rather dismal Saxon archer among the tightly massed English defending Harold's command post at the Battle of Hastings

The Battle of Hastings lasted throughout the whole of that short autumn day. The English tactics were to hold the shield-wall along the crest of the hill, beating off assailants by throwing javelins and engaging in hand-to-hand fighting. William's bowmen shot their arrows at the densely massed enemy, and the successive barrages must have been terribly effective against such an easy target. Next the infantry attacked and the knights made a frontal assault up the slope. The initial attack was repulsed and the Normans feigned flight, pursued by many of the English who mistakenly thought they had the enemy on the run. The Normans rallied, cut off and massacred the pursuing English and then made a second attack, repeating the same pattern. Up to the later phases of the battle, each arm—archers, cavalry and men-at-arms—had acted independently, and none had achieved a decisive result. A radical change of method was called for, and William applied the principle of co-operation. The archers were ordered to direct their arrows high into the air as a protective barrage for a final attack. This action has been criticized by several modern writers, but the simple fact is that in any case archers would have had to have shot at a higher elevation than normal, as they were shooting uphill at an enemy on a higher level. If, in addition, we assume that during the course of the battle the Norman archers had drawn back to the rear of their own army, it being natural enough for the cavalry to take the forefront, then they would have had to have shot higher into the air to gain the extra distance. As we shall see from later medieval battles, volleys of arrows descending *en masse* were far more effective in the height of battle than individually aimed shots. Then came the moment of ultimate disaster for the English defenders—King Harold himself was killed, and the defeat of an utterly demoralized army was only a matter of time.

Robert Wace, one of the most romantic of Norman authorities, describes at great length the arrows shot into the air and the resulting death of Harold: 'The Norman archers took their bows and shot swarms of arrows at their enemies, but the English protected themselves with their shields and

The scene wrongly associated with the death of Harold at Hastings. The juxtaposition of the word 'Harold' and the wounded soldier probably gave rise to the 'arrow in the eye' legend

none was actually wounded. No matter how carefully they aimed, no matter how skilfully they shot, the Norman bowmen did no damage to the English. Then they thought of the idea of shooting up into the air: as their arrows came down they would land on the Englishmen's heads, or hit them full in the face. They carried out this plan and shot their arrows high above their enemies. As the arrows came down, they fell on top of the Englishmen's heads, thudding into their skulls and faces, and even piercing their eyes, so that they were afraid to stick their heads out round their shields and some even kept their eyes shut. The arrows flew through the air thicker than the wind-driven rain. The English call them "billets" and the air was full of them. Then it happened that, as it whistled down out of the sky, one of these arrows struck Harold just above his right eye. In great anguish he dragged it out, snapping it in half and throwing it on the ground; but it had put his eye out. He was in great pain from this wound in his head, and he collapsed forward on to his shield. Among the English there is to this day a jingle which they often recite when they are talking to Frenchmen:

> ' "The arrow which struck Harold's eye
> Was straight and strong. Down from the sky
> It screamed, delighting all the French
> Who cheered to see blind Harold blench!" '

The story of Harold being pierced by an arrow in his eye is given in later writings only, and Guy of Amiens, writing less than two years after the event, gives a much more complicated and surgical account of Harold's death. He was, according to Guy and to several other writers, hacked to death by Norman knights, and patient modern research has confirmed this.

The principal evidence for the type of bow weapon used at Hastings is contained in the Bayeux Tapestry. This famous needlework chronicle was designed, if not actually fabricated, in Canterbury, England, to the order of Odo, Bishop of Bayeux. It was designed to be hung round a wall, probably in Bayeux Cathedral. Its purpose was to tell the story of the fall of King Harold and the triumph of William as graphically as possible to an illiterate people. The captions enhanced the understanding of those who could read Latin; no doubt they also served as running headlines for churchmen who were explaining the sequence of events to groups of visitors—very much in the way this is done today with the aid of portable recordings of the story in several languages. However, the tradition of the way in which Harold met his death, by a Norman arrow, is perpetuated in the popular tourist version. 'Why change the story, even though it's not correct,' retorted a present-day French guide when confronted with the more accurate account, 'after all it is what the public expect!' Thus the truth is set aside for the more acceptable, although apocryphal, version—after all the course of history cannot be changed by pedantic insistence for the accurate reporting of Harold's death, but at least the legendary skills of the Norman bowmen have been preserved by the more romantic story.

The bows depicted in the tapestry could well have been Saxon bows, familiar enough to local workers who may never have seen the improved models from the Continent. Robert Hardy, whose history of the longbow pulls together many loose ends, deals with the proportions of the archers in the tapestry and in particular the relative sizes of the bows they carry. He suggests that the difference in length between about half these bows is due to the fact that some of the bowmen are dismounted horse-archers who would be carrying shorter bows than the regular foot-archers. Other questions remain unanswered, such as the intriguing possibility that the short bows were of composite construction, and the longer bows were of the pattern which we have associated with the north-eastern European and Viking types.

Brigadier Barclay, whose admirable work on the event is significant from the military point of view, discusses the range of the bows used by the Normans, but his maximum estimate of 150 yards is not acceptable by those more experienced in the practicalities of archery. The bows which we believe to be the type which would have been used by the Normans could have had a range of 250 yards or more, and if there were, in addition, composite bows among the invaders' weapons, then their range could have exceeded this. An examination of the battlefield indicates that whatever weapons were used to fling the final volleys high in the air, they must have been very powerful, for the distances involved could have been up to 400 yards. One chronicler, who wrote in 1070 and whose accuracy is sometimes questioned by scholars, mentions the use of crossbows by

110

the invader. William could have known of the crossbow from his campaigns in the Near East, and it is therefore possible that at least some of his mercenary troops were so equipped. The fact remains that although the crossbow was in popular use in Europe during this period as a military weapon of great power, it never succeeded in replacing the hand-bow as the regular military weapon in Britain.

We have briefly mentioned the fact that the Norman army commanded by Duke William included mercenaries, and it is interesting to speculate on the possibility that among those hired troops there were those whose principal weapon was the composite bow. It is, of course, wrong to consider the invasion of England in 1066 in isolation from the rest of Europe when we talk of composite-bow-armed mercenaries. There was an active exchange of commerce, and movement of people and armies over the whole of Europe and the Near East by land and sea during this period, and the concept of 'national' armies was still remote. The pattern of mercenary service was fairly general and it was not restricted to national boundaries, although such boundaries in feudal Europe were largely undefined and constantly changing. William's force comprised two or three thousand knights, the hard core of his force, and in support there were three or four thousand infantry, volunteers and mercenaries, who would have been drawn not only from Normandy but also from all parts of France and even from the adventurers in southern Italy, where there was a Norman empire found by Robert Guiscard in 1053, and beyond. There is no doubt that the composite bow was common enough in the south of Italy and it would be feasible to assume that it was brought to Britain by mercenaries from there.

Certainly if we can believe Giraldus Cambrensis, who wrote his *Itinerary Through Wales* in 1188, there is good reason to assume that the composite bow was well known in Britain by the end of the twelfth century. He says '... the bows the Welshmen use are not made of horn, or ivory ...', which implies that he was familiar with those that were so constructed. Much earlier the composite bow was certainly known in Britain during the Roman occupation, being the weapon of the *Cohors Sagittariorum*. The whole question is intriguing, and there are many aspects which have yet to be unravelled, numerous gaps which have to

111

be filled with positive evidence yet to be discovered. There, somewhat regretfully, we have to rest our proposition which suggests that the weaponry the Normans brought with them included the composite bow. Its use during the battle would go far to explain the superiority of fire enjoyed by the Norman invaders.

Harold's army consisted of Englishmen who owed military service direct to the king. The employment of mercenaries by Harold seems doubtful as the chroniclers are silent on this point. The militia of the realm, the *fyrd*, which was recruited on the basis of one man for every 600 acres, was kept in readiness by the earls and the sheriffs and, when required, they could be called out to serve only for forty days at a time, but later allowance was commonly made for an extension at given rates of pay. There was, in addition, a class above ordinary freemen, known as *thegns*, who also were obliged to turn out for military service when required. No such thing as national standing armies existed, and the obligations of the militia included the provision of certain weapons and equipment which did not include the bow. Had that weapon been adopted previously as a general weapon in England, the outcome of the battle on Senlac Hill might have been reversed and the course of history altered. It was many years before the lessons of this momentous conflict were put into practice on the same scale as the example set by the brilliant generalship of William the Conqueror.

We have referred briefly to Giraldus Cambrensis—Gerald the Welshman—who accompanied Archbishop Baldwin, who was to preach the Third Crusade, through Wales. In his *Itinerary* he described the people of Gwenth as being 'more accustomed to war, more famous for valour, and more expert in archery, than those of any other part of Wales'. From their skilled use of the bow it has wrongly been assumed that the longbow, which gained final recognition as a weapon *par excellence* during the fourteenth and fifteenth centuries, originated in Wales. The Welsh of the twelfth century were a wild race, given to hasty acts of aggression, and we can read many instances of their impulsive actions producing reprisals to their disadvantage. William de Braose put to death a great number of Welshmen imprisoned in Abergavenny Castle in revenge for the murder of Henry of Hereford, after making an un-

It is interesting to speculate on the type of bow being used by this fourteenth-century Italian bowman. The recurved tips suggest a composite form, and the size indicates enormous power. The archer is clearly a warrior—probably from Tuscany

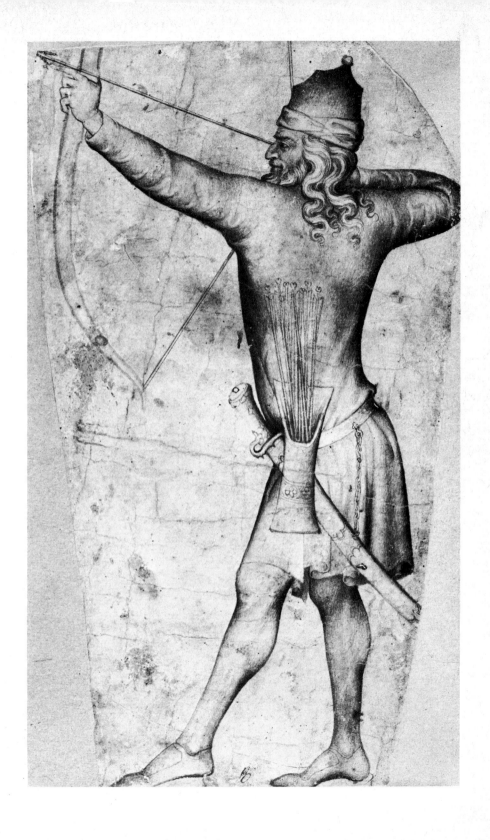

successful attempt to extract a promise, under oath, that none 'should bear any bow, or other unlawful weapon'. He realized that in the expert hands of a Welshman the bow was a weapon to be feared and respected, and so he attempted to outlaw it. This also serves to indicate the distinction which was beginning to be put on bows and arrows as 'official' or 'unofficial' weapons, and in a short time we shall see the legal development of this attitude.

The same William de Braose testified that one of his soldiers, in a conflict with the Welsh, was wounded by an arrow which passed through his thigh, the armour in which it was cased on both sides, through that part of the saddle which is called the alva, and mortally wounded the horse. Another soldier was pinned to his saddle by an arrow through his hip and the covering armour; and when he turned his horse round he got another arrow in the other hip that fixed him in his saddle on both sides. Giraldus, however, was not overimpressed by the courage of the Welsh in battle, which, he tells us, 'manifests itself chiefly in the retreat, when they frequently turn, and like the Parthians, shoot their arrows behind them'. Possibly the passage most quoted from the writings of Giraldus Cambrensis, and which illustrates best the power of these bows from Gwenth, concerns 'an oaken portal which was four fingers thick' penetrated by several Welsh arrows during a siege of Abergavenny Castle in 1182. According to the chronicler the bows were 'made of wild elm, unpolished, rude and uncouth, but stout; not only able to shoot an arrow to a great distance but also able to inflict severe wounds at close quarters'.

It was from castles in South Wales that, only a few years before the *Itinerary Through Wales* was written, Richard de Clare, Earl of Pembroke, set out with his Marcher Lords to invade Ireland in the last of the Norman conquests. His chain-clad knights were supported by archers, whose skill was then the speciality of Wales, and it was these campaigns which earned him the soubriquet of 'Strongbow'.

The first mention of the use of massed archery by the English comes from Sussex, where in 1216 more than 1,000 bowmen harassed the army of the Dauphin Louis and the rebel barons as they marched through the Weald. This little-noticed French invasion included a concept of war which was to have a major influence on the way battles were fought by English armies and how they developed the full potential of archery in European warfare.

The next landmark in the history of the bow in battle was the Assize of Arms of 1252. This statute directed that in a time of national emergency Commissioners of Array could select and impress men to serve as paid soldiers in the royal ranks. This was the beginning of a national standing army. After ordering that the richer yeomanry who owned 100 shillings in land should come to the host with steel cap, buff coat, lance and sword, the Act proceeds to command that 'all who own more than forty and less than a hundred shillings in land come bearing a sword and a bow with arrows, and a dagger'. Similarly, citizens with chattels worth more than nine marks and less than twenty are to be arrayed with bow, arrows and a sword. Even poor men with less than forty shillings in land or nine marks in chattels should bring bow and arrows. By these means England obtained a reserve of amateur soldiers upon which she was able to draw for service in all her wars until the threat of Napoleon. The Statute of Winchester of 1252 was the first official English recognition of the importance of the bow in warfare, a great advance which was to prove of inestimable importance during the next two or three hundred years; and it was a welcome contrast to the earlier Assize of Arms of 1181, which did not mention the bow at all.

It was in England also that a dramatic change occurred which developed the hitherto unused potential of infantry acting in co-ordination with cavalry, and the use of infantry as a decisive striking force. These principles had been generally ignored before the second half of the thirteenth century, and the princely tactician responsible for this military revolution was Edward I (1274–1307), conqueror of Wales, victor at Falkirk in 1298, a great military organizer and a fine commander. At Orewin Bridge (1282), Falkirk (1298) and Halidon Hill (1333), longbowmen defeated spearmen, and these battles were preludes to the even more decisive victories of Crécy, Poitiers and Agincourt.

Edward's campaigns in Scotland alternately succeeded and failed according to the manner in which the English army was handled by its leaders. The Battle of Falkirk was the first engagement of real importance in which the bowmen, properly supplemented by cavalry, played a leading rôle. Wallace had gathered all Scotland to his banner

115

and had withdrawn to the great forest of Torwood between Falkirk and Stirling. When King Edward received news of the proximity of the Scots he decided to press his famine-stricken army on towards the enemy. Eventually the English came in sight of Wallace and his army occupying a strong position on a hillside about two miles south of Falkirk. Their front was protected by a broad morass; the Scottish pikemen were arrayed in four great 'schiltrons', and behind them were 1,000 men-at-arms who composed Wallace's cavalry. On each flank and between the schiltrons were

War in France. Ambushed French are being pursued by the English, led by the Earl of Warwick, the crossbowmen proving no match for the longbows of the English. Early fifteenth century

several thousand archers armed with the short bow. Wallace had fully deployed his troops and was prepared for a thoroughly defensive battle.

Edward drew up his men in three 'battles', and almost immediately two cavalry corps began advancing simultaneously, skirting the morass from left and right in wide detours. These two masses of careering knights executed a headlong charge against each of the Scottish flanks. Wallace's archers were ridden down and scattered, and his 1,000 men-at-arms rode off the field without striking a blow for Scotland, but the great schiltrons of pikemen flung back the rush of horsemen. This was the decisive moment of the day and Edward was quick to grasp the situation. The knights were commanded to halt and the bowmen were brought forward. They were ordered to concentrate their fire on fixed points in the enemy masses, and very soon they began to make a fearful slaughter. Then the command came for the knights to charge for the second time, and the rest of the fight was little more than a massacre.

The lessons of Falkirk were simple and very similar to those of Hastings; that even the best of infantry, if unsupported by cavalry and placed in a position that might be turned on the flanks, could not hope to withstand a judicious combination of archers and horsemen. According to many historians Robert the Bruce served on the English side at Falkirk; whether this is true or not, he doubtless learned important lessons in strategy at this time which were to stand him in good stead at Bannockburn some sixteen years later. The Bruce taught the English a vital lesson at that battle, and later, on the fields of France, they showed, in their use of foot and archers in preference to the Gothic concept of a lumbering column of charging knights, how deep that lesson had been driven. 'Poitiers and Agincourt were won under the rock of Stirling,' said one historian, with very sound reasoning.

CHAPTER 6

War with France

Despite the notion that subsequent successes of English archers in battle were due to the hard lessons learnt at Bannockburn, 'under the rock of Stirling', the fact remains that their superiority during the Hundred Years War was due to a number of factors in addition to changes in strategy, which evolved as a result of the necessity of putting into battle large numbers of trained archers at short notice. In particular many of these factors were related to the control of the manufacture of weapons, their storage and distribution, the training of archers themselves and their terms of service. Neither must we forget the special qualities of their commanders, notably Edward III, the Black Prince and Henry V, who are particularly associated with the victories of Crécy, Poitiers and Agincourt. From the thirteenth to the fifteenth century England was in a virtual state of war with the Scots and the French, and the short periods between each active engagement were taken up by furious preparations for the next.

This period of English history is crowded with the complex claims of succession set against a background of intrigue and political manœuvre, a changing society preparing to throw off the yoke of feudalism and, one of the basic reasons for war, growing economic pressures, which demanded greater wealth and more territorial possessions. Individual fortunes were also to be made by participation in war such as those of Sir John Fastolf, who made enough money out of Henry V's French campaigns to build a castle at Caister, a house at Southwark, and manors all over England; in addition he partly endowed Magdalen College, Oxford, and still had enough money to spare to invest in the wool industry and lend to merchants. One mercenary admitted: 'Do you not know that I live by war, and peace would be my undoing?' For special services rendered rewards were given; the capture of a nobleman might lead to a share of the ransom, and even bringing news or information could result in a substantial gift. There were thus strong selfish reasons for keeping the pot of war simmering and for encouraging it to boil over from time to time.

This was an age in which the daily life of all classes of men were carefully recorded, not least the fourth estate, and by such reports we are able to understand more fully the conditions under which the ordinary soldier, and the archer in particular, served his king in times of war. In addition to being able to reconstruct the battles in which he fought, we can glimpse special incidents and brief moments which were his experience during those events. We have spoken of the pickings of war, which even for the humble soldier were considerable. For example, on the battlefield of Poitiers, some Cheshire archers picked up a silver ship, probably a large salt cellar, belonging to the French king, and the Prince of Wales bought it from them. Another incident, which brought what must have been a substantial

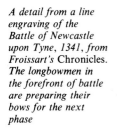

A detail from a line engraving of the Battle of Newcastle upon Tyne, 1341, from Froissart's Chronicles. *The longbowmen in the forefront of battle are preparing their bows for the next phase*

119

windfall to an archer named John Dancaster, was carefully chronicled by Geoffrey Baker, and it conveys the courage and resourcefulness of the principal character as well as his licentiousness, which was only to be expected from a soldier of an expeditionary force of the fourteenth century.

Following the successful siege of Calais, Dancaster had been captured by the French and, not being able to free himself by payment of the ransom demanded, was freed on condition that he worked amongst the French repairing the defences of the castle of Guines. Some of the occupying garrison of Calais meanwhile planned how they might overthrow the castle. Baker's chronicle goes on: 'This fellow Dancaster chanced to lie with a laundress, a strumpet, and learned from her where there was a wall two feet broad stretching from the ramparts across to the edge of a ditch so that, being covered with water, it could not been seen.... The archer (his harlot shewing it to him) measured the height of the castle wall with a thread.' John Dancaster then made contact with those who wished to capture the castle and by using the secret information he had gained they planned to occupy the fortress by stealth. The plan was carried out and '... they broke into the chambers and turrets upon the ladies and knights that lay there asleep, and so became masters of all that was within.' The raiding party then released the English prisoners held there and bargained with the Earl of Guines for the purchase of the stronghold. John Dancaster and his private army of thirty dare-devils, being true patriots, would only surrender the keys to the king of England, which they did, '... the King of England bought it, indeed, and so had that place which he greatly desired.'

Knowing the baser motives for war which motivated Dancaster, Fastolf and many others, it does not come as a surprise to learn that royal leaders themselves encouraged their armies by promises of such rewards. Before the Battle of Poitiers the Black Prince, judging the mood of his archers accurately, addressed them thus: 'Honour and patriotism and the prospect of rich spoils of the French, call you more than my words to follow in the footsteps of your fathers.' Prince Edward had an uncanny sense of the immortality his archers were to achieve; 'If envious fortune should decree, which God forbid, that in this present labour we must follow the final path of all flesh, your names will not be sullied with infamy and I and my comrades will drink the same cup with you.' This is the rousing stuff of which charismatic leaders are made, and apart from the royal recognition of the common bowmen, which was indicative of the Black Prince's regard for the archer, it also shows his awareness of the great necessity of boosting morale before a battle, particularly when the odds were against his gaining the day.

The morale of a modern army is the fruit of months and even years of training of officers and men. Fourteenth-century armies had little training or instruction, and archers, for example, were chosen, tested, arrayed, and their leaders appointed, only a few weeks before they would find themselves in a strange land as little more than an undisciplined armed mob. They then spent most of their time in looting, destroying and burning. Proper discipline must have been extremely difficult to maintain, and it is therefore the more remarkable that some sort of order was exercised over the various components of English armies, a mixed bunch which included Englishmen, Welshmen and foreign mercenaries as well as murderers and 'evil doers'.

Until 1160, English armies had consisted of local forces raised under military obligation to serve for forty days a year, and mercenaries hired from abroad. This system had two principal drawbacks. If a campaign were not over in forty days (and few were) large contingents of the army would melt away, despite the attraction of additional rewards from plunder and ransom. Secondly, the mercenaries, who were an expensive item, would only remain so long as there was pay or reward for them. Although these men were usually brave and loyal they were occasionally unreliable and dangerous, requiring to be paid above anything else. In 1160, when Henry II was engaged in a lengthy, though unimportant, war in Toulouse, he hit upon the idea of allowing knights to commute their military obligations for money. This was known as scutage (shield money) and had the advantage of providing badly needed capital to hire specialist troops, as well as enabling extra expenditure to be made on warlike materials and conveniently dispensing with unwilling soldiers. By 1337, 'the process of reducing the compulsive and increasing the voluntary element was carried still further'.

The obligations to muster when 'called to arms' by the

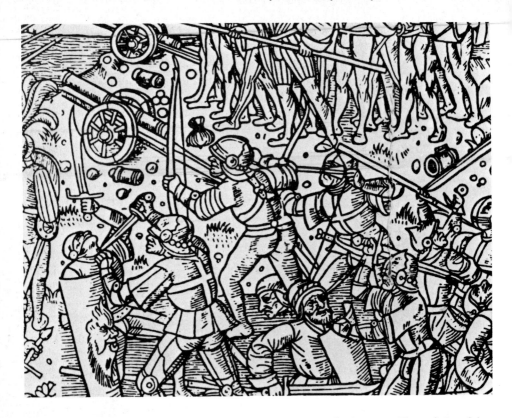

king's authority was the subject of numerous regulations, and the system, with variations, became the recognized method for supplementing a regular standing army in times of emergency. Precise instructions were issued from time to time for the manner in which archers were to present themselves when called upon, and the penalties for non-compliance were harsh. Each man had to bring a bow and at least thirty arrows fitted with suitable arrow-heads.

The confusion of the mêlée in this detail from the Battle of Fornovo, 1495, must have hampered the movements of archers caught up in battle. Note the coup-de-grâce being administered, probably by an archer who has discarded his bow after using all his arrows

> In special at the first moustre, every archers shall have his bowe and arrowes hole, that it to wytte, in arrows XXX or XXXIV, at the least, headed and in a sheaf. And furthermore, that every archere do sweare that his bowe and arrowes be his own, or his mastyr's or captyne's. And also that no man, ones moustered and admitted as an archere, alter or change himself to any other condition, without the kinge's special leave, upon payne of imprisonment.

These 'yeomen bowmen', as they were referred to by one chronicler, were described by Froissart as 'Milices redoutables! la fleur des archiers du monde.' (Formidable troops! the flower of the world's archers.)

In the 1340s recruitment by contract was widely used, and a scale of wages evolved that was applicable not only to the archer but also to the earl. Archers' pay varied at different times, but it steadily improved and reflected the extra skills that were required for this class of soldier. In 1281 the foot-archer received twopence a day, seemingly a pittance, but if comparisons are drawn with contemporary values this represented not an unreasonable remuneration. Six hundred and fifty years later, at the outbreak of the 1939–45 war, a private soldier's pay commenced at two shillings a day! In 1338, for the mounted archer at any rate, the wages were good. They were sixpence a day—the wages of a skilled, even of a master craftsman. There was also an additional payment or war bonus called a 'regard', which was paid over to the leader of a group once a quarter. One of the items in the accounts of Edward III reads, 'Paid to the sixty archers, for their wages, bows and arrows, and other necessaries, £30.' If this represented the statutory forty days' service then each archer received ten shillings, or threepence a day, a sum he was certainly receiving in 1346, the year of Crécy. The maximum daily pay of sixpence was paid to troops from Cheshire, those coming from Flintshire in North Wales receiving only threepence. 'There's many a good bow besides one in Chester,' goes an old saying, and it is interesting to speculate on the origins of such a statement. One wonders why the Welsh bowmen, so renowned for their archery skills, should receive less reward than those from Cheshire, and thus it is possible that the saying may have originated as a form of indignant Welsh protest.

The status and accomplishments of an archer appeared to have been held in high regard, and other trades and talents in the fourteenth-century expeditionary forces which had no place in the official establishment rolls were usually classed as archers. No doubt this also enabled suitably high wages to be paid to those who could not be otherwise accounted for. For example, in 1344, Edward III's army in France included a military band consisting of five trumpeters, one citoler, five pipers, one taborer, two clarioners, one nakerer, one fiddler and three waits, all ranked among the archers of the royal household. John O'Gaunt's *Register* of 1373 includes this item; '... whereas we have great need this next expedition . . . beyond the seas, of certain craftsmen . . . send four carpenters, two masons and two ironworkers to make and work engines and trebuchets and other such things . . . and so far as you can see, see that they are good archers, and suitable . . . and above the number of archers for whom we have already sent. . . .'

Although the 'voluntary element' became stronger in the early part of the fourteenth century, the 'compulsive element' was barely concealed by an invitation to volunteer by the end of that century, when the French threatened to invade England. A proclamation was made to the effect that those able and willing to go to the coast in defence of the realm and the City should report to the Guildhall to the Mayor and Chamberlain and receive their pay, viz: twelve pence per day for men-at-arms properly arrayed and sixpence for archers '...and any of those men-at-arms or archers who were able but not willing were to be arrested as traitors to the King and the City.' There was therefore little option and no chance of escaping 'voluntary' service in times of emergency.

The longbow was the prescribed weapon of the rank and file, and archers who carried it rapidly grew in numerical importance. For example, the Muster Rolls of the Arrays for 1339 for the various counties in England show that archers already formed exactly half the foot soldiery, and in later years this proportion increased. By the summer of 1386, when England was preparing to defend herself against the French, there were 100,000 archers ready to ward off invasion, apart from those on overseas campaigns. The supplies of bows and arrows for successive bodies of archers as they were mobilized were on an immense scale, and the sheriffs of towns and counties were ordered to supply certain quantities of warlike materials according to population and wealth. The year 1356 is a good example. In January, nineteen English counties were ordered to supply 6,200 bows and 9,900 arrows, and the following month a further 1,000 bows were supplied, plus 2,000 sheaves each of (say) thirty arrows and 400 gross of bow-strings. In March, the king commanded William Rothwell, Keeper of the Wardrobe, to conscript armourers, fletchers and bow-string-makers and set them to work as long as was necessary to provide the king with the munitions he required. Any

124

workmen showing themselves 'contrarious or rebellious' were to be imprisoned. In the December of that year a further 1,000 bows were purchased together with 10,000 sheaves of good arrows and 1,000 sheaves of best arrows (for the king's bodyguard), 100 gross of bow-strings, feathers of geese and other necessities for the fletcher's craft.

These and many other similar accounts reveal the vast quantities of bows and arrows that were made during the fourteenth and fifteenth centuries. A simple computation will show that in one year alone at least half a million arrows were provided, apart from those already stocked in the Tower of London and other fortresses, and discounting those for which no records survive. By the middle of the fourteenth century the City Guilds of Bowyers and Fletchers were established, and these livery companies carried out important functions such as guaranteeing standards of workmanship, pooling technical skills and resources, and operating the apprenticeship system. Profiteering was eschewed, although from time to time official warnings were given to the effect that suppliers of below-standard goods or those who charged inflated prices would be severely punished. Specifications for the making of serviceable arrow-heads were issued at the end of the fourteenth century, and other official orders were published concerning the type of wood to be used for arrows, controlling the cost of bows and encouraging the import of good bow-staves by waiving customs duty on staves longer than six and a half feet.

The medieval war effort was a well-organized affair, and the arrowsmiths and fletchers, bowyers and bow-string-makers, had three distinct methods of disposing of their products. They could produce their wares and sell them as independent craftsmen, they could contract to sell their goods at an agreed price, or, on occasion, they would be impressed to work at 'the King's wages'. Under the last arrangement William Lory, an arrow-head-maker of the fifteenth century, was paid the princely sum of fourpence a day. Arrows were tough, durable and cheap (in 1351 each arrow cost about a penny-ha'penny and in 1462 arrow-heads were five a penny) and, what was more important, they were in plentiful supply. Early types of military arrow-heads had a broad, flat blade with a prominent shoulder, but by the thirteenth century a more compact type had appeared—a logical reduction in size as a result of the development of body armour. The trend was to produce an arrow with more penetrative power, and the ultimate result was the infamous 'bodkin'—a square-sectioned, chisel-ended arrow-head capable of piercing the stoutest leather, fine mail and even plate armour. As an efficient weapon of war, capable of being mass-produced at low cost, the arrow proved itself over a long period. It was remarkably well made considering its expendability, and from the millions that must have been made there remains only one guaranteed medieval relic, thirty inches long, which was found in the Chapter House of Westminster Abbey.

We have spoken of the ancient bows that have been preserved dating back to the early centuries AD. There are, in addition, one or two bows from the sixteenth century onwards which we can examine, such as two of the bowstaves salvaged from the wreck of the *Mary Rose*, which sank in 1545, and the Flodden Bow, preserved in Archers' Hall, Edinburgh, traditionally associated with the battle of that name of 1513. The gap between these two groups of surviving bows cannot be filled with anything but conjecture as to the precise pattern of bows used in warfare from the thirteenth to the fifteenth centuries. However, we can state with some confidence, and with the help of contemporary description and illustration, that the English longbow at its best was a well-made and efficient weapon, made from yew and utilizing the unique mechanical properties of that wood of which we spoke earlier. Robert Hardy suggests that the absence of archery relics from the period of the Hundred Years War is due to the fact that they were common and familiar things, which were not hung up as trophies on the tombs of the great, nor buried with the ordinary men who were so skilled in their use. However the bow was not reserved exclusively for military use. At this time in practically every cottage and rural homestead there could be found a longbow, kept handy, possibly slung over the fireplace (the 'smoke stained bows' of which Thomas Walsingham spoke and which were carried by the mob who followed Wat Tyler in 1381), used for archery practice on Sundays and Holydays and ready for use should the menfolk be called out to serve the king in France. Another reason for the fact that none of these bows have survived, suggests Robert Hardy, is that after constant use wooden bows will

126

weaken and break, and once a bow was no longer serviceable it would be thrown away or used for firewood as there would be no possible reason for preserving it. Nevertheless it is a source of wonder that a dozen or so bows and a few sheaves of arrows have not survived in some dark and dusty loft or cellar of one of the many stronghold storehouses that were used as military depots at that time.

The Wound Man. *A gruesome reference chart used by medieval surgeons to identify different types of wounds likely to be encountered in battle*

The medieval arrow could inflict terrible wounds, and if an arrow did not immediately kill its victim it usually meant eventual death if the warrior were struck in the upper body or head. In addition, once the arrow had found its mark in a horse, the rider would be thrown and he would then become vulnerable; if he were wounded there would be the risk of being killed on the spot by foot soldiers with knives and mauls. Surgery was practically unknown, and even if it had been developed to the high science of today, the life of the stricken man hardly could have been saved under field conditions, because even modern surgeons regard the extraction of an arrow from certain parts of the human body as an almost fatal operation. One legal account, prepared at the turn of the fourteenth century, deals with an enquiry into the murder of Simon de Skeftington; it records how he received a fatal wound from an iron arrow-head tipping a thirty-three-inch shaft of ash shot from a yew bow five feet seven inches long. The wound measured three inches long by two inches wide and was six inches deep, a

A crude but effective method of removing a barbed arrow-head. Whether the victim of this primitive surgery recovered is not known, but this method remained standard practice until the nineteenth century

terrible gash testifying to the effectiveness of medieval archery.

The protective clothing of the bowmen in the English armies was often limited to a leather jacket, which sometimes had plates of iron on the breast and at the elbows. A few archers, usually those who were mounted, had chain hauberks, and the cloth jackets of others were lined with mail, but the majority were without armour. Many wore a steel or chain skull-cap, or a conical hat made of boiled leather. Writs of the middle of the fourteenth century commonly state that the troops raised in a given county are to be clothed 'in one suit', at the county's expense. The writs state no reason for adopting uniform and, except in one limited region, they do not mention the colour, size or form of the suit. In the records of Cheshire and Flint there are details of the clothing of the archers and of the Welsh lancers. In these two counties the material used was woollen, the articles supplied were short coats and hats, and the colours were green and white—green on the right side of both articles, white on the left, ordered for every group of men raised in this period.

To be fully armed, paid and arrayed was one thing, but training in the use of those arms was another. To ensure that the entire male population, with few exceptions, were kept fully trained during peacetime in preparation for war, a series of Statutes of the Realm were promulgated ordering archery practice. The earliest law of interest concerning archery was passed in the reign of Henry I, and absolved an archer from charges of murder or manslaughter if he accidentally killed a man while practising. This is the first official encouragement for archery known in Britain, and it set the pattern for others to follow from time to time confirming the official desire for a well-trained reserve army of bowmen.

From the reign of Edward I every village in England contributed to a national pool of archers, every yokel being commanded by law to practise at the butts on Sundays. Edward III, knowing the value of such training, encouraged it by royal proclamations, insisting on regular archery practice under pain of fine or imprisonment. An example of such a statute was the one directed to the sheriffs of the counties of England in 1369, which read, '... cause public proclamation to be made that everyone of the said city London,

Battle scene from the Chronicle and Conquests of Charlemagne, probably typical of the countless engagements in which men-at-arms, bowmen and cavalry fought at very close range

strong in body, at leisure times on holidays, use in the recreations bows and arrows ... and learn and exercise the art of shooting; forbidding all and singular on our behalf, that they do not after any manner apply themselves to the throwing of stones, wood, iron, hand-ball, foot-ball, bandy-ball, cambuck or cockfighting, nor such other like vain plays, which have no profit in them or concern themselves therein, under pain of imprisonment.'

From such a well-trained potential, in underpopulated medieval England, it was thus possible to assemble thousands of skilled bowmen, who were to enjoy a remarkable military superiority, and who followed their king to France to claim back disputed possessions for the 116 years that historians have labelled the Hundred Years War.

The factors that precipitated two great nations into a long, expensive and wearying war were complex. Described by Froissart as a series of plundering expeditions by four generations of Englishmen, this conflict between England and France was never really concluded. No general peace treaty was signed and the English king did not formally renounce his claim to the throne of the Valois and the Bourbons until the Peace of Amiens in 1802. After several years of argument, claim and counter-claim, threats and defiance, England and France slowly lumbered into war, and our story begins with Edward's invasion of France in 1340.

Edward III's army set sail across the Channel, and the first notable action of the war was fought at sea off Sluys, a battle of nine hours, the course of which was to pave the way to the conquest of France. Forty thousand men awaited the arrival of the English fleet, including massed Genoese crossbowmen and men-at-arms, filling upwards of 120 vessels and outnumbering the English by four to one. King Edward's ships fairly bristled with archers who, shooting from the ships at long range, cleared the shores and covered the invading troops. 'This battle was very murderous and horrible,' said Froissart; 'archers and crossbowmen shot with all their might at each other and the men-at-arms engaged hand to hand. . . .' The *Christopher*, which had been taken from the English the year before, was recaptured and the English 'manned her again with archers, and sent her to fight the Genoese'. The French fleet was defeated, and the following day the English king landed quietly in Flanders, ambitious and confident, and prepared to do further battle after having gained the first victory of the Hundred Years War.

For several years there was intermittent warfare on the frontiers of Gascony, without any decisive result, during which the archer gained in stature as a fighting man. From the experience of Scottish wars the army chiefs of Edward III had shaped a new method of warfare, combining the archer and the feudal knight in a single unit of battle, formidable alike for its missiles and its sword-play. When the archer's true value became fully recognized he was often supplied with defensive armour and a horse, so that the whole army of mounted infantry could scour through France on their raids. But all from king to scullion would dismount to fight if the occasion demanded.

In the spring of 1346 the English army was reconstituted, and new, carefully chosen levies, including 12,000 archers,

130

The fate of the rock-throwing soldier in the crow's-nest demonstrates the penetrative power of English longbows in this battle at sea

landed at St. Vaast in Normandy in July. The landing was forced under the cover of a rain of arrows which, once more, drove off the massed crossbowmen lining the quays of Cadzand Haven. There was a sharp fight on shore and the archers were posted on the flanks to protect the main body. The Bastard of Flanders charged the English, but was com-

131

pletely routed by the irresistible hail of arrows from the flanks. The object now was the capture of Paris, and the English army thrust on to St. Denis, where they were repulsed by the whole might of France. The retreat of Edward's forces over the Somme, where at Blanchetaque his archers again proved more than a match for the unfortunate Genoese crossbowmen, was the prelude to what Churchill has described as one of the four supreme achievements of the British Army—the Battle of Crécy.

It is possible to stand today on the very mound used by King Edward as his command post, and the course of the battle of 26 August can be plotted over fields that have hardly changed since 1346. The mound, on which there was a little windmill, stood on a low ridge facing south-west between the villages of Crécy and Wadicourt. Behind lay a wood, the Bois de Crécy-Grange, which, with the forest of Crécy on the right, provided cover in case of need. The ground sloped gently towards the Vallée aux Clercs and to a track that led from the wood to the south-east, still known as Le Chemin de L'Armée, along which the French army would presently advance.

More than half of Edward's 13,000 men were archers, added to which he could count on some 3,000 knights and men-at-arms. The marshals deployed the latter in three divisions, two of which were stationed a little way down the forward slope of the ridge, the remainder being held in reserve. The archers, with Welsh spearmen in support, were arranged as four projecting salients on both flanks of each of the two forward divisions. The formation was described as a 'herce' or harrow, from its rough similarity in pattern to that implement. In front the archers hammered in iron-pointed stakes and dug pot-holes to protect themselves from cavalry. Such a formation was calculated to force the attackers into two narrowing gulleys, where they would have to contend with the English armour while being raked by arrows from the flanks.

The sixteen-year-old Prince of Wales, later more familiarly known as the Black Prince from the black cuirass he wore at this battle, who had just received the accolade of knighthood from King Edward, was in titular command of one of the divisions; before the day was out he was to undergo his first major experience of battle and learn a military lesson that would eventually be put to good advantage

The English and French at the Battle of Crécy. In this nineteenth-century engraving, a view from the French position, the English reserves are seen just below the windmill, Edward III's command post

when he commanded his own army. When all was ready the English waited and watched the vast French host slowly appear and take up their positions in the Vallée aux Clercs. The French army outnumbered the English by three to one and careful estimates give us a total of 40,000 men made up of men-at-arms, mercenaries, foreign notabilities and their personal followers, and the provincial levies. The mercenaries consisted mainly of some 6,000 crossbowmen from Genoa, who had already suffered heavily at the hands of the English archers during the past two days' fighting.

The vast French column moved on without proper control. The divisions were never properly sorted out from the start, still less towards the end of a long march, and contradictory orders of changes of direction, countermanded and then repeated, resulted in complete disorder. King Philip took command and, expecting the arrival of reinforcements, decided to halt while his footsore and weary main body rested and reorganized. But his commands were only partly obeyed. Impulsive French knights, supremely confident, ignored the order and pushed forward. The Genoese, who were in front, were jostled forward and had no option but to advance on the English in a hopelessly ragged formation. They slowly crossed the valley and started to ascend the slope until they were about 150 yards from the point where the English still waited. Here the story is taken up by Jean Froissart in his lively chronicle: 'During this time a heavy rain fell, accompanied by thunder and a very terrible eclipse of the sun; and before this rain a great flight of crows hovered in the air over all the battalions, making a loud noise; shortly afterwards it cleared up, and the sun shone very bright; but the French had it in their faces, and the English on their backs. When the Genoese were somewhat in order they approached the English and set up a loud shout, in order to frighten them; but the English remained quite quiet and did not seem to attend to it. Then they set up a second shout, and advanced a little forward; the English never moved. Still they hooted a third time, advancing with their crossbows presented, and began to shoot. The English archers then advanced one step forward and shot their arrows with such force and quickness that it seemed as if it snowed. When the Genoese felt these arrows, which pierced through their armour, some of them cut the strings of their crossbows, others flung them to the ground, and all turned about and retreated quite discomfited.

'The French had a large body of men-at-arms on horseback to support the Genoese, and the king, seeing them fall back, cried out, "kill me those scoundrels, for they stop up our road without any reason". The English continued shooting, and some of their arrows falling among the horsemen, drove them upon the Genoese, so that they were both in such confusion, they could never rally again.'

Assault after assault was launched by the French and a bitter hand-to-hand battle took place, but the English stood firm, the archers sending vast numbers of arrows into the mêlée and the Welsh and Cornishmen creeping forward with knives to butcher great numbers of dismounted French knights and men-at-arms who were wounded or rolling helplessly amid the press in their heavy armour. The English knights stood their ground and inflicted great losses on those of the enemy who managed to break through to their lines. Soon after midnight the bitterly disappointed French king, himself wounded in the face by an arrow, was persuaded to leave the field, admitting the utter defeat of the might of France. Fifteen or sixteen assaults had failed, and the flower of the chivalry of France lay dead on the field of battle. The remainder of the French melted away in the darkness; but there was no pursuit, for the English king, who had never once lost grip of the battle, had forbidden his men to break ranks. While the English losses were astonishingly light, the French were said to have lost 10,000 including no less than 1,542 knights and men-at-arms and eighty standards.

Just ten years after Crécy the Black Prince again defeated the French, this time at Poitiers, in another example of a relatively small number of men confronted by overwhelming odds—in this case about eight times their number. The Black Prince was desperately anxious not to fight, for his men, laden with plunder after a long *chevauchée* through Berry and Limousin, were obviously exhausted. His retreat had been halted by the French, who blocked his way to Bordeaux, and escape to the south was impossible. Fortunately the Prince had the benefit of advice from that gifted veteran Sir John Chandos, a soldier of genius, who selected an ideal defensive position just south of the town of Poitiers. The English had time to take up their positions and spent the whole day frantically improving their defences, making 'great dykes and hedges about their archers'. The engagement started with the launching of about 300 chosen mounted French knights towards the hedge that protected the English front. The archers, safe behind this hedge, shot steadily 'and did slay and hurt horses and knights'. German mercenaries who were supporting the French were driven off when a body of archers came out from far along the hedge and, protected from heavy troops by standing in marshy ground, shot murderously into the enemy flank.

The fighting became fierce and the supply of arrows started to dry up, and 'archers even pulled arrows out of enemy wounded who were only half dead'. For a while it seemed that the situation worsened; for although the English archers, 'moved to fury because they were desperate', shot better than ever, the French managed to ward off the arrows by holding shields over their heads. The battle was now on open ground in front of the hedge from behind which the archers, who had used up their last arrows, came out with swords and axes to help their men-at-arms. Suddenly the banner of St. George was seen behind the French. The Prince had sent sixty men-at-arms and 100 archers down a hidden track, through a hollow, which came out behind the enemy. This had the effect of breaking the French formation and they began to leave the field and surrender. 'You might see many an archer, many a knight, many a squire, running in every direction to take prisoners,' writes the Chandos Herald, while 'there were divers English archers that had four, five, or six prisoners', records Froissart. Fortunes were made from ransoms, as well as from the loot that was to be found.

The French were subjected to constant defeats by the indomitable longbowmen and understandably they sought some form of defence from this terrible weapon. Increased body-armour was soon penetrated by new designs of arrowheads, and the once invincible cavalry charges were rendered impotent by the slaughter of horses in full tilt, which fell victims to arrows with vicious, heavy points of steel. The French king, Charles V, began to emulate the English, as he could only surmise that their successes could be reversed if their own methods were used against them. He began to pay his troops more regularly than hitherto, no more ransom money was sent to the English, and he raised finance

The tombstone of William le May, Captain of the Corps of Archers of the King, and Governor of Paris in the fifteenth century

from special taxes. Over a number of years the French king issued imaginative edicts dealing with military matters, and eventually he had a permanent force paid for by the new revenues. The machinery of muster and review, which controlled soldiers' pay, was tightened up to stop commanders claiming money for non-existent troops. Townsmen were ordered to practise archery so that they could help in defending their own walls. This resourcefulness, plus a policy of scorched earth and guerilla raids, seemed the only effective way of countering the English combination of archers and dismounted men-at-arms in a direct confrontation. There was also the fact that generally the French refused to fight a pitched battle even when the odds were in their favour.

So the Hundred Years War dragged on, son following father at the butts to practise the skills of archery, each likely to be called up at any time for service overseas, each learning how to lay his body in the bow to coax the maximum length from each shot. The interminable expeditions and the consequent drag on the social structure of England by the incessant drain on resources of manpower and materials began to take its toll, and Richard II, recognizing this war-weariness and anxious to enable the reserve of archers to be kept up to standard, ordained that no servant or labourer should have any arms other than bows and arrows. They were to practise with them on Sundays and they were to stop playing their favourite games. In addition the authorities kept a watchful eye on bowyers, stringers and fletchers, as the safety of England depended on the availability and the reliability of their wares. Henry IV had trouble with arrowsmiths who made broadheads of inferior metal, and during Richard III's reign at least one stringer was brought to court to answer for his 'false and deceptive bow-strings. . . .'

The rivals and successors of the arbalesters who had been employed by the kings of France, particularly during the Hundred Years War, were the *francs archers*. They were created by Charles VII between 1448 and 1451, and he ordered every parish and every fifty households in the realm to provide a fully equipped bowman, armed with the familiar longbow, the weapon that had been so successfully used by the English. Each bowman was selected by the alderman of the parish from among those skilled in the use of the bow,

137

and regular training sessions became an obligatory condition of sevice. On active service he was paid four francs a month and he was exempt from certain *tailles*, both feudal and royal. He had to be ready to depart at a moment's notice at the king's command.

The exemption from taxes caused these soldiers to be called *francs* or 'free'. They did not have a proper uniform and assembled in companies of four or five hundred men under the command of a nobleman. They fought in the later stages of the Hundred Years War, at Formigny in 1450, and Castillon in 1453. Louis XI disbanded these bowmen in 1479, the year they disgraced themselves at the battle of Guinegatte, but his successors, Charles VII and Louis XII, used them again. Francis I reorganized them and in 1552 established them in a legion. They were finally suppressed during the reign of Charles IX.

A curious incident involved one such *francs archer*, serving under Louis XI, who had been condemned to death for a crime long since forgotten. This soldier deserves a special niche in the history of medicine, for he agreed to undergo an experimental operation by a surgeon who wanted to try his hand at removing gallstones, with a promise from the king that if he survived the surgeon's knife he would be set free. The first operation for gallstones was carried out in the year 1474, in the charnel house of the ancient church of Saint Séverin in Paris; the archer survived, and earned his freedom.

CHAPTER 7

Agincourt and after

Over half a century after Poitiers, on Passion Sunday, 1413, Henry V was crowned King of England and France and Lord of Ireland, in Westminster Abbey. Very soon it became clear that he was beginning to deceive himself into the fixed belief that he was the rightful heir to the throne of France. He followed his star with unfaltering courage. This arrogance, this sublime faith in his own triumphant destiny, protected him from ever realizing the futility of his conquests, which were indirectly to lose his own son the throne of England. Henry V will always go down in history as a great soldier. His own sense of destiny did not hamper his actions or muddle the decisiveness of his thoughts. 'Fair stood the wind for France'—now was the time to claim the heritage of the English throne, and Henry, reviving Edward III's pretensions to the French crown, set sail for Normandy in the year 1415.

Earlier the King had quietly prepared for the invasion of France while he pretended to negotiate with the Burgundians and Armagnac. France was broken by civil war while these two great factions seesawed in and out of power, and each had offered various proposals to Henry in answer to his territorial and sovereign claims. While ambassadors passed from country to country, arrows and bows were being cut at top speed in London, barrels of brimstone were being stored in Poultney's Inn and at the Tower, and smiths were casting cannon. Every kind of steel instrument with which a man might maim or kill his fellows, every kind of ram, tower, pontoon and engine was being made. Ships

139

were being repaired and built, oaks were being felled, nails and rigging prepared, foreign ships stolen and impressed. Writs were issued to master craftsmen, sheriffs and land-owners ordering the supply of every warlike commodity. Such an order was sent to Nicholas Frost, bowyer, who was to provide, at the King's charge, workmen to make and repair bows and to collect wood from any place he liked except from land belonging to the Church. Frost, together with five other bowyers and a group of fletchers, eventually accompanied the expedition to France as part of the King's retinue of specialists, tradesmen and personal household.

The French expected the invasion at Boulogne, but the King had secretly decided to make for Harfleur, an impor-tant port at the mouth of the Seine within striking distance of Paris. Following a brisk engagement, not without serious loss to the English, the port of Harfleur fell to Henry, but the plan to advance on Paris became extremely hazardous due to a combination of various factors, and the King's War Council strongly recommended the return to England of the whole army. The season was getting late for campaigning: the King of France was assembling an army in the Paris-Rouen area which was likely to be formidable in numbers, and dysentery had taken a terrible toll of the English army. After a proportion of fit troops had been allocated to garri-son duties at Harfleur there were only 900 men-at-arms and 5,000 archers available for field operations. Despite the recommendations of his council Henry decided to march on Calais, hoping to avoid interception from the French national army which was marshalling in the area of Rouen. A gruelling seventeen days followed during which time the English army marched no less than 260 miles, while march-ing more or less parallel with them, crossing and recrossing their route, was the bulk of the French forces. Then, on the eve of St. Crispin, the English came across the French host bivouacked astride the road to Calais, just short of the little village of Agincourt.

The French forces are estimated to have totalled at least 25,000. They were in high spirits and, although they had marched nearly the same distance as the English, the majority had been on horseback and were therefore much fresher. They now faced the weary and dispirited English army, most of them hungry and many still suffering from dysentery. They faced each other over a field newly sown with wheat. This open space, bounded by the woods of Agincourt on one side and Tramecourt on the other, narrowed towards the English positions, which had the effect of compressing the French as they advanced, restricting their movements and creating confusion and disorder.

There were three divisions of the English, on either side of which were groups of archers thrown forward and outwards, somewhat like an opened triangle. When these divisions were drawn up flank to flank in one line the archers met, forming a series of wedges. English morale was momentarily raised to an unexpectedly high level by the King, whose powers of inspiration and leadership had never been more advantageously displayed; he now rode along the lines on a little grey horse, wearing a magnificent suit of shining armour and a surcoat embroidered with the leopards of England and the fleurs-de-lis of France. His harangue to the assembled troops included a reminder that the French had boasted that they would cut three fingers from the right hand of every archer they might capture in order that they might never presume again to shoot at man or horse. Four long hours of waiting passed, both armies holding their ground, the English bowmen becoming restless and impatient. As the morning wore on Henry's confidence began to waver. He had hoped to fight at dawn, or soon after, for his men would be incapable of fighting the following day being very much wearied with hunger, diseases and marching.

The decision to take the initiative was soon made after a brief council of war between the King and the most experienced of his commanders. Edward Duke of York came to Henry and suggested that stakes should be planted before the archers, and accordingly every man took a stake of a tree and prepared it by sharpening it at both ends. Sir Thomas Erpingham was told to ensure that the archers were in their right positions. They were dirty and ragged, as well as hungry and tired. Their loose jackets were torn and mud stained; many of them were barefoot, and some of them, according to one account based on uncertain authority, were naked, without even the hat of boiled leather, and wearing only a belt in which their arrows and clubs were stuck. When they were all arranged to Sir Thomas's satisfaction he threw his baton into the air and cried 'Nestroque!'—interpreted as either 'now strike' or 'knee

141

stretch'. Sir Thomas was answered by a loud shout from the archers, and a few minutes later the famous order 'Banners Advance!' rang out and the divisions moved forward, slowly, steadily and firmly, in fine order, with trumpets sounding, and shouts of 'St. George!' ringing through the autumn air. The shrewd Henry had detached a body of 200 archers and sent them behind the English army by a circuitous route to a concealed position in a meadow not far from the village of Tramecourt close to the French vanguard, with orders to lie low until the time for action came. At extreme bow-shot the advancing army came to a halt; the archers planted their stakes in front of their forward ranks, and started to shoot. Suddenly the 'air was darkened by an intolerable number of piercing arrows flying across the sky to pour upon the enemy like a cloud laden with rain'. This was probably calculated to provoke the French into advancing, and it had the desired effect. The cavalry lumbered into life and decided to charge the flank archers according to plan, and as they started to advance the men-at-arms also moved forward, probably without orders. The knights galloped forward bravely, keeping their heads down so that the arrows, which came flying towards them in a continuous stream, did not hit them in the exposed part of the face, and they rode straight at the fence of stakes. Those horses that were not impaled on the stakes were so infuriated by the arrows that tore deep into their flesh that they became unmanageable. Some leapt backwards, stung to madness, some reared hideously, some turned their backs on the enemy and others merely fell to the ground throwing their heavily armoured riders at the feet of the archers, who stabbed or clubbed them to death. In the meanwhile the small body of archers concealed on the flank were harrying the enemy from their left wing, and by the time the two armies met in hand-to-hand battle the French were so closely packed that they could not raise their arms to strike the foe. During the general mêlée which ensued the ranks of archers stood their ground and poured shower after shower of arrows into the tight mass of the enemy. The result was complete disintegration of the French army, the whole action taking little more than three hours. Their casualties, which included 'the flower of all nobility of France', are said to have been between ten and fifteen thousand compared with the English dead of a few hundred. The

The Siege of Tournai, 1340, in which the English, with their allies from the Low Countries, attacked the French who improperly occupied the town. Used enemy arrows are being collected to be shot back into the town

tragic order given by the King to an esquire and 200 archers, to cut the throats of all prisoners, was to be remembered long after the event. In the heat of battle Henry had received news that his baggage camp had been attacked, added to which the French who had fled from the fight were re-forming ready to counter-attack. There was, therefore, a serious threat that he might lose the battle if the enormous number of prisoners already taken were to rejoin these re-forming units. So the King chose their wholesale extermination as a safeguard, an order carried out with much reluctance and considerable misgivings. Despite this instance of cruel butchery the personal record of King Henry was a shining example of individual bravery and valour, a historical fact which is incontestable. When the battle was over, Henry asked what castle it was that he saw in the distance through the veils of rain that had begun to fall on the gruesome field, and he was told that it was Agincourt. 'Then,' he said, 'let this day be called the Battle of Agincourt.'

143

Successive English kings not only had the problems of the Hundred Years War to contend with abroad, there were also the troubles with Scotland at home which appeared to be interminable. Again it was claims for the throne and the cause of independence which dominated the causation of this endless conflict; questions which continue to smoulder today. Many of these troubles manifested themselves in skirmishes and sometimes exploded into set-piece battles, and the resultant circumstances became confused and dangerous and encouraged even further conflict. Several battles fought on English and Scottish soil during this period are of interest from our point of view, as they not only demonstrate the importance of the archer in battle but also show that it was not only in France that the home-bred talents of English bowmen were used to advantage.

One typical example is the Battle of Halidon Hill of 1333, which has gone down in romantic history as King Edward's revenge for Bannockburn. Edward III was besieging Berwick when a powerful Scottish army suddenly appeared to deliver the town. Edward took up a position on a hillside with marshes below and a wood on its brow. His knights were ordered to dismount and to form up in line with the archers and other foot soldiers. The Scots were forced to attack, as Berwick could not be relieved unless the English were beaten in the open field. They came lumbering down the opposite hillside in four great columns. The marsh at the bottom forced them to slacken pace and they began to slowly climb Halidon Hill. Their progress was halted by a terrible storm of arrows and all the front ranks went down together. The following troops strove to push forward, but each party as it emerged from the chaotic mass was promptly shot down, and it seems that very few Scots managed to struggle up as far as the English men-at-arms on the crest of the hill. The final stage of the battle was a rout. Edward's knights remounted, charged the remnant of the Scottish army and pursued them for five miles—the day was his.

Halidon Hill was the second, as Dupplin Moor was the first, of a long series of defensive battles fought against the Scots, and won by the skilful combination of archery and dismounted men-at-arms. Neville's Cross, Homildon, Flodden, Pinkie, are all variations upon the same theme. At the first-named fight the archers so riddled the Scots' left wing that it broke up when attacked by the English men-at-arms, and left the centre bare to flank attack. At Homildon they so teased the Scottish masses by careful long-range shooting that they came storming down from a strong position (like Harold's axemen at Hastings), and were caught in disorder and completely dispersed by the main body of the English as they strove to pursue their assailants. In the main, the features of Flodden and Pinkie belong to the same class as Dupplin, Halidon, Homildon and Neville's Cross. The moral of all is the same; although the Scottish pikemen were invaluable against cavalry, they were helpless against a combination of bow and lance. In many ways one can detect a parallel with France in the way the Scots pursued their strategies by avoiding general engagements, their harrying of the land before the advancing enemy, and the confining of offensive action to ambushes and night surprises—'the wyles and wakenyngs of the night', as was laid down by King Robert I, the victor of Bannockburn.

During their oft renewed strife with England the Scots found good cause to dread the superiority of their old enemies in the use of the longbow and it is therefore not surprising that enlightened men in the north, in company with their allies the French, tried to encourage archery. However, these efforts were in vain. For want of old tradition and hereditary aptitude Scotland never bred a race of archers such as those who flourished in England. James I, for example, realizing the paramount importance of archery, endeavoured by every means in his power to encourage the practice of it among his subjects. 'That all men busk themselves to be archers, from the age of twelve years; and that in each ten pound worth of land there be made bow-marks, and specially near parish churches, where, upon holydays, men may come, and at the least shoot thrice about, and have usage of archery; and whosoever uses not the said archery, the lord of the land shall raise from him a wedder; and if the lord raises not the said penalty, the king's sheriff or his ministers shall raise it to the king.' And '... yeomen of the realm betwixt sixty and sixteen years shall be sufficiently provided with bows and sheafs of arrows. ...' It is clear, however, that the Scots preferred the games of golf and football to acquiring dexterity in the use of the longbow by shooting at the butts: '... the futball and the golf be utterly cryit doune' and 'that bowe marks markis be made ... and shuting to usyt ilk sunday.'

On 21 July, 1403, was fought 'the sorry battaille of Schro-
vesbury between Englysshemen and Englysshemen', described by a French chronicler as 'a battle unparalleled in
history'. It was certainly one of the decisive battles of the
Middle Ages, deciding which should be the reigning family
for the next sixty years. Henry IV had marched north with
his army, having agreed to help the Earl of Northumberland
to repel the Scots. By the time he reached Burton he was
dismayed to learn that the Earl had turned against him and
had taken sides with the Welsh chieftain Owen Glendower,
and that they planned to join forces with the Earl's son,
Harry Hotspur, in the vicinity of Shrewsbury. The King's
son, later to become Henry V, was dangerously isolated at
Shrewsbury with a force that had been carrying out a raid
in North Wales. There was but one course open to the King;
he must march with all speed to the help of his son, and
this he did, just in time to prevent Hotspur from breaking
into the town.

The two armies drew up in full view of one another, but
beyond bow-shot, on the ground now known as the Battlefield, and after a pause during which the Abbot of Shrewsbury failed to negotiate a peaceful settlement, they engaged
one another with the longbow. As soon as the King's
archers came within range the skilful bowmen from
Cheshire let fly their deadly shafts; the royalists answered
in kind but, after a fierce exchange broke ranks and
streamed away down the hill. Hotspur, quick to see his advantage, sent his men-at-arms in pursuit. A general mêlée
ensued, during which the Prince received an arrow in the
face; and a little later in the course of this indescribable confusion, Hotspur, perspiring with the heat of battle, raised
his visor for air and fell, his brain transfixed with an arrow
sped by an unknown hand. The news spread, with the inevitable result; the rebel line gave way and they quitted the
field. While 'the dead lay as thick as the leaves in Autumn'
a merciless pursuit of the survivors was launched by Henry,
and the victory was complete.

From the eleventh to the fifteenth century many soldiers
saw in archery the decisive weapon; and this vast cavalcade
of kings and princes, armoured knights and men-at-arms,
and bowmen from the English shires and the Welsh marches
in their hoods and liripipes, illuminate the pages of history
with a special lustre. Millions of arrows must have rotted

James I, King of Scots, in an unfamiliar rôle. His interest in the military application of archery is symbolized by the ceremoniously held bow and sceptre-like arrow

away, their carefully wrought points doomed to rusty extinction and their grey goose and peacock fletchings now nothing but dust. The sturdy yew bows have withered and disintegrated. But the passage of time cannot dim the glory of the victories they won for England or the cruel memory of civil battles.

William I, the ruthless conqueror, whose son was to die by the same weapon that gave his father England, moulders

147

in Gothic splendour at Caen. Edward I, during whose reign the longbow first became prominent as a weapon of war, caused the following inscription to be placed on his tomb in Westminster Abbey: *Edvardus Primus, Scotorum malleus hic est, 1308*—'Here is Edward I, Hammer of the Scots'. So great was his yearning to conquer Scotland that he required of his son that his bones were to be carried in a leather bag at the head of the English army till Scotland was subdued. The third Edward, the tactician supreme, one of the greatest princes who ever sat the English throne, whose sword and shield that went with him to France once formed part of his monument in Westminster, rests now in the Confessor's Chapel in that Abbey. The Black Prince, whose terrible name was used by generations of French-women to quiet their disobedient children, sleeps in the great cathedral at Canterbury, his tomb adorned with the plumes of the tragic blind king of Bohemia who fell at Crécy; and Henry V—sometimes called the first modern general—lies in Westminster, the legendary helm 'that did affright the air at Agincourt' hanging in the darkness above, still showing the fearful marks made by the great sword of the Duke of Alençon. The arms of France and England con-join in the achievements of these and other princes, as a permanent reminder of the long and bitter struggle between these two great monarchies.

Many hundreds of other knights, encased in sepulchres of stone, ride their spectral steeds for ever on clouds of glory. And the bowmen? They lie in mass funeral pits where they fell, covered, perhaps, with rough grey and brown and green coarse-spun hoods and capes, easily identifiable in the aftermath of battle, their fingers calloused from the con-stant friction of the bow-strings and their faces tanned from long months of hard campaigning. Their eyes were once bright and keen to spot and fix a target at 240 yards; their spirit was unquenchable, their loyalty unshakeable. They obeyed without question the commands of their lords and princes, and found in the interminable expeditions to a strange land a spirit of adventure, pride and self-reliance which was handed on from generation to generation. Ignor-ant, bawdy, simple countrymen; yet this was a class of soldier as noble as any history has known. The mobilization of home-bred talents, and the introduction and skilled use of archery, secured for the English victory after victory and

148

Archers of the mid-fifteenth century in battle during the Wars of the Roses, from an aquatint of 1812

established a pattern of warfare never before known, and never defeated by a weapon of that time. The lessons of Hastings and Bannockburn had been well learnt, and the place of the longbow in the history of military arms was to be challenged only by the rapid improvement in the entirely new science of firearms.

However, before the bow reached its final demise as a

149

weapon of war, England found herself again embroiled in various warlike involvements, not the least being the Wars of the Roses. The English garrisons and armies had returned home to a country torn by unrest and rebellion, conditions that soon fermented into the bitter conflict between the houses of Lancaster and York. The discontent in England had manifested itself in uprisings such as the Kentish rebellion of Jack Cade, a soldier home from the wars, who led 20,000 men to London after opposing Henry VI's army at Sevenoaks. The towns and villages of England were full of knights and archers accustomed to war and plunder, and fit for any mischief. The rival claimants to the throne, Edward of York, descended from Edward III, and the Red Rose of Lancaster, Henry VI, found ready support for their causes. The issue was simple, but the various factors which encouraged men to take sides were complex and confused; the stake was the throne of England, and the balance of power depended on the two great armies massing for civil war.

After the wars with France, rebels and vagabonds wandered the land and used the weapon of the common man for any illegal venture such as poaching, murder or revolts

The conflict that burst over England in such battles as St. Albans, Barnet, Towton, Edgecot, Losecoat Field, Wakefield, Mortimer's Cross, Tewkesbury, Bosworth, Hedley Moor and Hexham, were fought by the sons and grandsons of those same soldiers (and, perhaps, by some of the men themselves) who once stood side by side at Agincourt. Now they faced each other, equally armed with the weapon they had used to such advantage during the past two centuries. The tactics of these battles were those employed by the leaders in the recent French war; the archer still fought on foot, in line beside the man-at-arms, and the longbow was still the lord of weapons. The men involved consisted partly of mercenaries and partly of tenants and private friends hastily called out. Every country gentleman kept in his pay a number of soldiers, and the services of archers were in great demand. Sir John Howard, contracting for the services of such a bowman, a man named Daniel, offered him £10 a year, two gowns, and a house for his wife to dwell in. As an extra inducement he gave Daniel a shilling, two doublets worth five shillings each, a new gown, and sent him off to a shooting match with twenty pence more jingling in his purse. The dignitaries of the Church, long acclimatized to sudden and violent action against their safety, likewise thought it expedient to arm;

Bishop Wayneflets, for instance, stored at Farnham Castle amongst other irreligious implements 'large barbed arrows, with peacock's plumage'.

The first of the battles of the White and Red roses was fought at St. Albans in 1455, in which the Lancastrians were defeated, Henry VI taken prisoner and Richard Duke of York, who claimed the throne by descent from Edward III, placed at the head of the governing power. Richard was killed at Wakefield, and his son proclaimed himself Edward IV. The Battle of Towton, which was fought in a blinding Yorkshire snowstorm in 1461, gave Edward his first great victory over the Lancastrians. The first incident of this battle was the capture of Ferrybridge by Lord Clifford, nicknamed 'Black Clifford', and its recapture by the Yorkists, following the death of that bloodthirsty nobleman by a chance arrow finding its target in his neck. The main action was fought by two large armies, both well disciplined in arms. The Yorkists, taking advantage of the snow, which was driving into the faces of the enemy, shot a flight of arrows into their ranks and then retreated a few paces. The Lancastrians, thinking their foe nearer than was the case, plied their arrows fast and thick against the blinding snow with no result whatever, except to exhaust their quivers. Now the Yorkists replied and poured into the enemy a deadlier shower of arrows, their own store supplemented by those which had fallen harmlessly at their feet. The remainder of the battle was fought for a gruelling eight hours at close quarters, and it was equally balanced until the arrival of reinforcements for Edward's army; once they arrived, fresh and enthusiastic, the scales were weighed against the Lancastrians, and the battle ended in victory for the usurper.

Now, with the reigns of Henry VIII and Queen Elizabeth, the bow was to suffer a long and lingering decline, and a battle of words between adherents of the bow and supporters of the gun, unparalleled in the history of military writings, was to begin.

151

CHAPTER 8

Bow versus gun

Among his continental military ventures Henry VIII invaded France three times, although the only action at which he was present was the Battle of the Spurs. While he was thus engaged the French king tried to stir up the Scots to attack him in the rear. This resulted in the last general action ever fought by an English army consisting only of the traditional 'bows and bills'. On 9 September, 1513, three weeks after the Battle of the Spurs, the battle of Flodden Field was fought on the Northumbrian border. In many ways Flodden marks the end of an epoch. It is significant both from the tactical and strategic point of view as being the last on record of the fights between men on foot which had been so common in the fifteenth century. Up to this time battles had been fought in great blocks of troops, the 'vaward', 'main-battle' and 'rearward', and now this concept had been replaced by smaller and more numerous units. It also differs from its predecessors in that archery played a secondary rôle in the decision. Whether the tactical changes resulted from design or by accident is not for us to question, but it is interesting to ponder on the question of the use of archery in that battle, and in particular whether a more aggressive use of this weapon—if indeed that had been possible—would have materially affected the outcome.

The cause of this conflict centres on the efforts of James IV of Scotland to weaken the power and cripple the resources of England in the approaching war with France. It is difficult to understand the quality of judgement which plunged two nations into a war for such reasons; the possibility of defeat or even the loss of manpower and resources appeared to have been completely ignored by the Scottish king. In the event the casualties on the Scottish side almost pass belief; the most moderate Scottish chronicle puts them at 5,000, while English authorities double that figure. Half the Scottish peerage roll were killed, ninety clan chiefs perished, and whole generations were cut off simultaneously—occasionally three or four brothers or cousins fell together. The fate of the unfortunate James of Scotland was discovered with some difficulty, for his body had been stripped like those of his company. He had been wounded by one or more arrows and had soon been cut down by deadly blows from English bills; his head was so hacked that he was hardly recognizable. James paid the full price for his ill-considered strategy and his lack of judgement cost Scotland dear.

Apart from the crippling arrow wound that King James

A detail from a painting of the Battle of Portsmouth, 1545, in which English bowmen are preparing to embark. Originally at Petworth House, the painting was destroyed by fire

had suffered (similar to that of Harold at Hastings), which proved effective enough to render him helpless in the face of the close-quarter hacking and chopping from English billmen, archery at Flodden has been lightly dismissed by chroniclers. However, the evidence suggests that the Scottish chances may have improved had they not been harried by the volleys from the English archers, and there remains the possibility that they could have thus gained the advantage. The other intriguing possibility is that James himself may have survived to fight another day had not a stray or a deliberately aimed shot contributed to his end.

King James, with a vast host of 100,000 eager and excited husky clansmen, crossed the border and laid siege to the castles of Norham, Wark, Etal and Ford. In the meantime the English had amassed a large army, and by means of emissaries, spies and treachery had made themselves masters of every detail concerning the Scottish army and their movements. By early September the Scottish and English armies were comparatively close to one another, and after some movements of troops to gain advantageous positions the two mighty armies faced each other about half a mile apart and with fronts stretching to about a mile and a half wide.

Eventually the trumpets sounded for the charge; the guns on either side opened fire with great vigour, but without any serious injury to either party. Hand-to-hand encounter soon began and one section of the English were driven back before the terrible rush of Highland steel and the landsknecht-type spears of the borderers. At this first attack the English suffered heavy losses, and after rallying again and again, only to be repeatedly repulsed, they finally wavered and fled. The attempt by the Scots to consolidate their advantage failed when a body of cavalry was brought in to reinforce the weakened English division.

Hour after hour every inch of ground was fiercely contested, neither side yielding nor gaining any appreciable advantage over the other. During the four hours of fighting it is clear that the contribution made by the English bowmen was of little more than a nuisance value, hampering the enemy rather than halting them. This was due mainly to the fact that the Scottish front ranks in particular were 'most assuredly harnessed'—that is in complete armour— 'and abode the most dangerous shot of arrows, which sore them annoyed, but yet except it hit them in some bare place, did them no hurt'. Ten days after the battle Bishop Ruthal wrote that 'they were so well cased in armour that the arrows did them no harm', and the contemporary *Treue Encounter* declares that 'few of them were slain with arrows'. It is not clear whether the English ran out of arrow supplies at an early stage, or whether they were quick to realize the ineffectiveness of their archery at short range against the heavily armoured enemy. Whatever the cause, the archers of Cheshire and Lancaster, under Sir William Molyneaux and Sir Henry Kickley, soon threw down their bows and joined in the general mêlée with sword and bill. It was a deadly struggle while it lasted, but gradually the clansmen gave way, fighting at first, but then suddenly in complete rout. Among the Scottish dead were the archers of Ettrick, who perished almost to the man. They were known in Scotland as the 'Flowers of the Forest', and to this day the sad, wailing air known by that name is invariably the Dead March used by Scottish regiments.

There is a considerable amount of evidence of the details of this battle, including the composition of the opposing armies, their weapons, contemporary commentary and chronicle, and even names of those who took part. The bowmen were still specially regarded and they were occasionally employed in proportions outmoded by the advent of new weapons. For example, Thomas Howard, when he was Earl of Surrey, conducted the victorious campaign at Flodden with a personal retinue of 500 men, among whom were 462 'bows and bills' under 'ten petty captains'. They were all in uniforms of green and white, an echo of earlier custom, and they accompanied Surrey to fight with him at Flodden, receiving ninepence a day for their services. The levies from the north which poured in to join Surrey included billmen and bowmen, many of whom were 'horsed and harnessed'. Their mounts were country hacks, which were sent to the rear in time of battle. With the exception of the cavalry support, both armies at Flodden fought on foot, and the close-quarter combat that developed gave little scope for long-range weapons. Against an enemy massing for attack, particularly those on horseback, barrage after barrage of arrow-shot proved to be deadly. Used as a tactical support weapon in enfilade or to weaken particularly dangerous enemy concentrations, archers could be used to great advantage. But once a battle had developed into a mêlée, archery proved to be useless, a situation that persisted from the onset at Flodden. None the less there must be some significance in the fact that in commemoration of the battle of Flodden the Earl of Surrey, the English commander, was given the honour of displaying the demilion of Scotland pierced through the mouth with an arrow.

Some doubts as to the continued use of the bow were already being heard, and one of the earliest doubters was Lord Herbert of Cherbury, who asked whether the previous successes in battle could be expected again, especially 'since the use of arms is changed and for the bow, proper for men of our strength, the caliver begins to be generally received, which, besides that it is a more costly weapon and requires a long practice, may be managed by the weaker sort'. These misgivings as to the efficiency of the bow in battle were laid aside, particularly when the first act of Henry's reign required every male (except ecclesiastics, judges, and people possessed of land to the value of two hundred marks a year) over seven and under sixty years of age to practise archery, the use of crossbows and handguns being forbidden.

The suppression of the monasteries by Henry VIII had caused considerable unrest in various parts of the country, and a general feeling of alarm and discontent prevailed. It was with the country in this unsettled condition that Henry, who placed great reliance on the support of the City of London, set his seal to the Charter that incorporated for all time the Guild or Fraternity of St. George, for the better defence of the realm by the maintenance of 'The Science and Feate of Shooting' with longbow, crossbow and handgun. This was the first body in England to receive official encouragement in the use of the handgun, and this company of élite soldiery was eventually to become the Ancient and Honourable Artillery Company of London.

Elizabeth appointed a commission to move about England to supervise the use of the bow 'which was much decayed', and William Harrison included an enthusiastic defence of the skill of the English archer in his *Description of Britain*. 'In the past the chief force of England consisted in their long-bows. But now we have given over that kind of artillery.... Certes, the Frenchmen and rutters [German cavalry], deriding our new archery in respect of their corslets, will not let, in open skirmish, if any leisure serve, to turn up their tails and cry: "Shoot English!" and all because our strong shooting is decayed and laid in bed. But, if some of our Englishmen now lived that served King Edward the third in his wars with France, the breech of such a varlet should have been nailed to his bum with one arrow, and another feathered in his bowels, before he should have turned about to see who had shot the first.' Harrison then grudgingly admits the new-found skills: 'But, as our shooting is thus in manner utterly decayed among us one way, so our countrymen wax skilful in sundry other points, as in shooting in small pieces, the caliver, the handling of the pike, in the several uses of which they have become very expert.'

The Elizabethan bowman and his equipment is admirably described in a contemporary manuscript: 'Captains and officers should be skilful of that most noble weapon [the bow]; and to see that their soldiers, according to their draught and strength, have good bows, well nocked, well stringed, everie string whippe in the nocke, and in the myddes rubbed with wax, braser and shutting glove, some spare strynges, trymed as aforesaid; every man one sheaf of arrows, with a case of leather, defensible against the rayne, and in the same fower and twentie arrows; whereof eight of them should be lighter than the residue, to gall or astoyne the enemie with the hail-shot of light arrows, before they shall come within the danger of their harquebuss shot. Let every man have a brigandine or a little cote of plate, a skull or hufkin, a maule of lead, of five feet in length, and a pike, and the same hanging by his girdle, with a hook and dagger; being thus furnished, teach them by musters to march, shoote and retire, keeping their faces upon the enemy's. ... None other weapon maye compare with the same noble weapon.'

The troops that William of Orange took into the field during the Dutch War of Independence were mostly composed of foreign auxiliaries such as English, Scottish and German infantry and German and Huguenot cavalry. The Dutch themselves concentrated more on naval service, a fact which materially determined the fate of the Invincible or Most Happy Armada of Philip of Spain. This threat was just as dangerous to Holland as it was to England, and while Dutch squadrons persisted in a blockade, the English were dealing with the high-seas fleet. The English forces at sea still included a complement of archers, and their methods had changed little since the days of the sea battle of Sluys two and a half centuries earlier.

Alexander McKee, in his book *Henry VIII's Mary Rose*, has reconstructed the moment of battle when two great warships met in fearful combat; huge unwieldy vessels packed tight with men and weapons, veritable floating fortresses. 'The approach of an enemy carrack would be a terrible sight. Its commander would intend, if he could, to strike one's own ship bodily, thrusting the great, overhanging bow castle over the low waist of the vessel. That bow castle could be many storeys high, looming larger and more formidable for every long minute of its approach. There would be the noise of the wind and the sea, the creaking of the ropes, the last-minute shouted orders to try and avoid the collision, the rolling and pitching of the deck and then, just before the shock, as the enemy's fore castle reared up above like a wall, from it would come the howl and whip of loosed arrows and the whispering sigh as hundreds of shafts shot to their target, turning the deck into a bloody shambles of screaming, groaning, writhing men. Volley after volley would search out the living from the dead and when the deck was a slaughterhouse, then, and only then, would the armoured infantry leap down on to it to attempt the physical conquest of the ship.'

'The fight was very cruel, for the archers of the English part and the crossbows of the French part, did their uttermost,' wrote Holinshead of the sea battle off Brest in 1511, and Cardinal Wolsey, writing of the same battle, said, 'Our men so valyently acquyt themselfe that within one ower fygth they had utterly vanquyshyd with shot of gonnys and arrows the said caryk, and slain most part of the men within the same.' There was a crucial difference between a fight at sea and a land battle. Fighting instructions to commanders stressed as late as the seventeenth century the inadvisability of giving quarter because any large body of prisoners might retake the captured ship. Therefore if you were on the losing side there was little likelihood of survival. The later engagements included, as an overture, great broadsides from muzzle-loading cannon, but the rôle of the archers remained the same.

In a contemporary account of a naval engagement off the coast of Britain during the wars with France in the year 1523, the desperate situation of the English, heavily outnumbered by the French, is vividly described. Particular emphasis is placed on the use of archery as a defensive measure; as long as there were arrows to shoot the attack was held, but once the archers had exhausted their quivers they were overwhelmed by superior odds.

'The nineteenth day of January 1523 six fair ships of France well appointed, met with a ship of the King's of England, called the *Katherine Galley*, a ship of forty ton, the Captain whereof was one John Mariner, with a small company, for many of his men were a-land: But he so encouraged his men that all fear was set aside, and ever as the Frenchmen approached, they beat them off with arrows, pikes, and fighting, and still this continued from four of the clock in the morning till nine of the clock, and ever on the coast of England, and the Englishmen did the best they could to save themselves:

'For by that time she had spent her powder; arrows with shooting, and her bills with hewing, and her pikes with keeping them off from coming aboard, and all the company almost sore hurt, and the Captain wounded to the death, so that they had no other remedy but to sail.

'This chase was perceived by one called Captain Markham, captain of the *Bark of Sandwych*, which manfully called his men together out of Sandwych haven and with good wind came to rescue the *Katherine Galley*. The six ships perceiving that, left their chase and made with the *Bark of Sandwych*. The Captain courageously comforted his men and made the quarters of his ship defensible. The Frenchmen set on fiercely, and their tops were higher than the top of the English ship. Out went the ordnance, quarrels, and darts of the French ships: the Englishmen shot fiercely again, and when the Frenchmen proffered to enter, the Englishmen bear them off with bills. The Frenchmen at last, with a great gun, beat down the top of the Bark, and slew the men in the same, and lastly they strake down his Mast. This conflict continued from ten of the clock till two after noon.

'Then he could make no shift but to sail: and ever the Englishmen shot arrows, and while the Englishmen had any arrows the Frenchmen durst not enter: But when their arrows were spent, the Frenchmen came abroad all at once and entered the Bark. In this fight were slain of Frenchmen out of hand twenty seven, and eighty sore hurt, and of the

English were slain twenty three. What should I say? The Englishmen fought valiantly, but they were too weak for six tall ships. Wherfore they were taken and brought to Deep [Dieppe] for a prize, but the Frenchmen said they never bought prize so dear.'

Among the warlike stores aboard the *Mary Rose*, which sank in 1545, and in addition to all the infantry weapons, there were 350 bows, 700 bow-strings, 700 sheaves of arrows and 200 'stakes for the field'. The latter were about six feet long and had sharp iron-tipped points at both ends, so that by thrusting one end into the ground at an angle a body of archers could very quickly surround themselves with an obstacle lethal to cavalry. This is a reminder that these ships were designed to provide both the bombardment and assault force in amphibious operations, as well as for fighting at sea.

To combat the threat of invasion from the Spanish Armada the shire levies were called out, and although by 1588 the bow was virtually obsolescent the contemporary muster-rolls include a fairly high proportion of archers. The scale laid down for a company of 250 men raised in Lancashire for 1584, for instance, was composed of eighty men with fire-arms, eighty pikes, forty halberds and forty bows. There were some regions where of all the men embodied there were no bowmen—only pikes and arquebusiers or caliver-men. This was the case in Cambridgeshire, Huntingdonshire, Wiltshire and Somerset. In London not one of the regular trained bands had a bow, but among the 4,000 supplementary untrained men 800 were scheduled as archers. In the Midlands and the North the proportions of bows to fire-arms ranged down from one-third to one-fifth, but was always in the minority. Only in the two forest counties of Buckinghamshire and Oxfordshire was there a slight preponderance of archers over arquebusiers.

The slow decline of the use of the bow in warlike situations continued throughout Elizabeth's reign, not without controversy between the admirers of the old weapon and the modernists who condemned it. A long familiarity with the weapon the English had made very special was difficult to set aside, and the threat of invasion by an enemy equipped with more modern weaponry did not deter enthusiasts, such as Lord Willoughby, from loyalty to outmoded defence measures. His adjuration to his troops, called out as an Elizabethan equivalent of the Home Guard, has a Churchillian ring: 'Stand to it noble pikemen, and look you round about, and shoot you right you bowmen, and we will keep them out.'

Although England could not keep out the arquebus, the caliver and the musket, the persistent loyalty to the bow is one of the most striking examples of conservatism in English history. What lay behind it? Free from invasion and not involved in most of the wars which forced the rest of Europe to keep abreast of developments in the art of war until late in the sixteenth century, Englishmen could afford to let tradition and sentiment affect their choice of weapons. The bow was the weapon of the patriot, with which the pride of France had been toppled at Crécy, Poitiers and Agincourt. Then there were the various vested interests which favoured the bow. The bowyers and fletchers, naturally, did not want their trades to suffer and they stressed the superiority of their own products over the musket and ball. Arrows were cheap, and could be used in practice over and over again, while the ammunition for guns, to the despair of local authorities, literally went up in smoke.

The great controversy between the admirers of the old weapon and the modernists who condemned it now began in earnest. The most important advocate of the bow was Sir John Smythe, who published in 1590 *Certain Discourses ... Concerning the Formes and Effects of Divers Sorts of Weapons, chiefly of the Mosquet, the Caliver, and the Longbow; As, Also, of the great Sufficiencie, Excellencie, and Wonderful Effects of Archers*. His critical observations on the comparative performance between bow and gun were answered by *A Brief Discourse of Warre* published the same year by Sir Roger Williams. These two books contained the essence of the argument which other writers took up, but it must be admitted that the theme of many of these military authors was somewhat backward looking. 'The myghte of the realme of England standyth the moste upon archers,' said Sir John Fortescue, and the following lines by Alleyne indicate the stubborn persistence of yet another historian convinced of the bow's superiority:

> That the white faith of Hist'ry cannot shew,
> That e'er the musket yet could beat the bow.

Humfrey Barwick, a brother officer of Sir John Smythe,

calling himself (in the title page to his book) 'Gentleman, Soldier, Captain et encor plus oultre', wrote an impatient reply to Sir John's observations on the use of the bow in which he declared: 'that he had held conference with divers persons, of sundry callings ... wherein he found so many addicted to the opinion of Sir John Smythe, touching the commending of the archery in England ... that many were thereby persuaded, that the long bow is the only weapon of the world for the obtaining of battails and victories.'

The main advantage of the bow, it was said, was that it would shoot several times faster than the gun—six aimed shots a minute, claimed Smythe, against only one from an arquebusier. The supporters of the gun claimed that the impact of the bullet was much greater than that of the arrow. Bows were more accurate, declared the archers, and the very sight of arrows darkening the sky struck terror into the enemy's heart. The art of archery is much decayed and archers can be as nervous in battle as arquebusiers, replied the followers of the gun, and the real efficiency of the bowman depends on the bodily strength, 'if he have not his three meals a day, as is his custom at home, nor lies warm at nights, he presently waxes benumbed and feeble, and cannot draw so as to shoot long shots'. At least, said the archers, they could not be blinded by smoke or put out of action by the least drizzle of rain as was the musketeer; after all, they continued, the bow is a simple weapon and firearms very complicated things—the piece clogs and fouls very easily, is liable to breakage, and can only be repaired by a skilled gunsmith. Wet weather spoils the powder, windy weather blows out the match, or sends its sparks flying among the powder of horns or bandoliers. If bad weather is pernicious to firearms, came the retort, it is no less so to bows. Rain makes bow-strings slack and after a march in the wet arrow-feathers flake off.

So the argument went on. There were even attempts to bring the bow up to date by devising new methods of using it; William Neade suggested equipping a 'Double-Armed Man' with a bow attached to a pike, and another inventor made lavish claims for flaming arrows ignited by a fuse, which was lit just before fitting them to a bow. In the dedication to his book Smythe charges Leicester and others of the Queen's advisers with incompetence and corruption. These charges were brought to the Queen's notice, and she

Highlanders on the march. A lively detail from an unrecorded print of the sixteenth or seventeenth century

directed that all copies of the book be 'called in, both because they be printed without privilege, and that they may breed much question and quarrell'. Sir John was sent to the Tower a year or so later and kept there for two years for using seditious language and inciting some of the musters to mutiny.

The modernists had their way, and the verdict was finally given against the bow when the Privy Council, by their Ordinance of 1595, decided that archers should no longer be enrolled in the trained bands as efficient soldiers, but only arquebusiers, caliver-men or musketeers; all bows had to be exchanged for muskets and calivers, and vast stocks of bows, arrows and archery appurtenances found their way into dusty stores in the Tower of London and other armouries. This was the virtual death-knell of the bow as a military weapon in the hands of the English, although there are some isolated instances of archery being used up to the middle of the seventeenth century, when bodies of archers were raised for service during the Civil War. Such instances are military curiosities rather than significant historical events. For example, in 1644 Lord Kilport commanded the bowmen who were on the left of Montrose's army at the battle of Tippermuir, and archery was said to

163

have been used at the great clan battle fought between the laird of Macintosh and Macdonald of Kippoch.

The story of the levy of Highland bowmen who arrived too late to join in the battle can be mentioned as a wry post-script to the history of the longbow in war. Whatever the cause it is certain that the bow continued to be made use of in the Highlands long after it had been forgotten in England and the Lowlands. Accordingly it is not altogether sur-prising to discover that a levy of Highland bowmen was raised for the purpose of serving under the Duke of Buck-ingham, which ended in the disastrous retreat from the Isle of Rhe in 1627. King Charles II granted a commission to Alexander McNaughton to raise a body of 200 bowmen, with an amnesty to any of them who were 'fugitive from our laws for criminal causes'. NcNaughton had problems from the beginning, he complained of the 'trouble and charges' he had in making up his company, and the journey to Falmouth was not without its discomfort: 'God knows how we have been tossed up and down by seas and storm of weather and chased by men of war.' Proper clothing had not been supplied and McNaughton complained that his men—'poor soldiers who are far from their own country', several of whom had stolen away by night—would be improperly dressed in their trews and blue caps. The final blow, wrote McNaughton from Falmouth, was that 'con-trary winds and frosts will hinder us long here', and his levy arrived too late to join in Buckingham's invasion of France. If, as it is most probable, this handful of men were destined to act against cavalry, and if they were to have been well supported by other troops, they might have proved useful; but otherwise they would hardly have failed to be an encumbrance to a modern army. The fate of McNaughton's Highland Archers is not known, but it is probable that they joined some of their countrymen in the German wars, and distinguished themselves under the banner of the heroic Gustavus Adolphus.

For years to come the occasional lone voice was raised in defence of the bow in the forelorn hope that it would again be in the front rank of the English armies. Gervase Markham, writing in 1634, suggested that archers should be brought back into the trained bands; the Earl of Crau-furd early in the eighteenth century recommended the adop-tion of archery in the British army as 'an advantage to these nations', and as late as 1776 Benjamin Franklin, in a letter to Major-General Lee, proposing the reintroduction of the bow into the American regular army, says, 'I still wish, with you, that pikes could be introduced, and I would add, bows and arrows: these were good weapons not wisely laid aside.' He gives the usual reasons for his opinion adding, as further advantages, the accuracy of the bow, the absence of smoke, and the ease with which bows can be procured.

For more than three centuries the longbow had proved its worth as a versatile weapon of war. The way of handling this bow so that the maximum efficiency could be coaxed from its limbs became exclusively an English attribute, and although other nations tried in vain to emulate these talents, they never quite reached England's level of command of longbowmen *en masse*, or their individual prowess, which resulted in major classic victories and countless minor ones. A strong affection developed between the Englishman and his longbow which reached deeper than just a regard for it as a weapon of war or of the chase. It became enshrined as a special symbol, and the men who used it became featured in legend and folktales. Particularly powerful are the memories of Agincourt and Crécy, and the heroes of these and similar battles have more than once reappeared to aid their descendants in military service in times of extreme stress and reversed fortune in battle.

A cry for supernatural help to a guardian angel, to a special god of war, or a favourite saint, is not unusual. One curious example of unsolicited aid centres round the tales of visions which appeared on the battlefield during the retreat from Mons in the First World War, published by Arthur Machen and admitted, by him, to be completely of his own journalistic invention. These stories aroused enormous interest, and encouraged Harold Begbin to collect eye-witness accounts of actual 'sightings' to answer Machen's claim and to prove that these stories were, in fact, not without some truth—that is for those who believe in the unexplained phenomena of human experience. One of these stories was told by a Catholic officer in a letter from the front. 'A party of about thirty men and an officer were cut off in a trench, when the officer said to his men, "Look here; we must either stay here and be caught like rats in a trap or make a sortie against the enemy. We haven't much of chance, but personally I don't want to be caught here."

165

The men all agreed with him, and with a yell of "St George for England!" they dashed out into the open. The officer tells how, as they ran on, he became aware of a large company of men with bows and arrows going along with them, and even leading them on against the enemy's trenches, and afterwards when he was talking to a German prisoner, the man asked him who was the officer on the great white horse who led them? for although he was such a conspicuous figure, they had none of them been able to hit him. I must add that the German dead appeared to have no wounds on them.'

Another story concerned a Colonel Shepheard who, as a staff colonel in the 1914–18 War, travelled from Haze- brouck to Wimereux. During his journey he swears he saw the grey hooded archers of Crécy looming up in the mist. 'Hooded, cloaked figures of silent, gazing men—rank beyond rank. There were thousands of them—all cloaked and hooded like monks. They rose slowly and every man stared fixed at me. It was a queer, wistful, sad stare, like a dumb question or a dumb warning. Their cloaks were grey, almost luminous, with a fine silvery bloom on then like moths' wings. I seemed to touch one and it came off on my fingers like a soft dust. Then slowly they sank back into the ground—rank after rank of hooded men sinking into the earth, their eyes fixed on me to the last!'

CHAPTER 9

Redskin warpath

No primitive man on earth ever fired the imagination of the fiction writer as did the American Indian. From the romantic novels of the nineteenth century, in particular, he has emerged as an athlete, skilled hunter, statesman, orator, warrior, relentless enemy and staunch friend, able to endure with unflinching fortitude hunger, cold—even torture to the point of death. The 'noble savage' became a stereotype figure allocated to one of a dozen or so of the more popularly known tribes, his monosyllabic existence enlivened by pow-wows, war dances, festivals to the innumerable deities of his pantheon of pagan gods, and poker-faced interludes while peace-pipes were passed around. Above all, his performance with a bow and arrow was regarded as superlative. The legend that has grown up around the Red Indian is not easy to dispel.

The first Americans arrived, so we are told, some 20,000 years ago after the first Ice Age man crossed the narrow bridge of land that almost certainly connected Siberia and Alaska (now the Bering Strait), and migrations and infiltrations from Asia started which continued for thousands of years. No one knows how many times America was 'discovered' by peoples of the Old World, and perhaps the last of these nomads arrived only a few centuries before Columbus; but it is certain that at some time during these continued migrations the bow was brought to the New World and, undoubtedly, the bow-using habits of these wandering tribes were gradually adapted to the new environments into which they found themselves settling.

167

The migrations that dispersed themselves over both North and South America gradually fragmented into a multiplicity of language families, and became grouped according to widely diverse patterns of living. Each of these groups evolved its own individual culture, which was adapted, modified or improved according to its location, hunting methods, domestic habits and many other factors; and eventually a vast pattern of the aboriginal American Indian emerged, speaking upwards of 500 languages and pursuing many cultures of enormous diversity and individuality.

Among the scores of tribes who lived in the vast region of the great forests were the Chippawa of the cold northern woods and the Atlantic seaboard tribes such as the Massachusett, the Peguot, the Mohican, the Delaware and the Powhatan. Close to the Great Lakes were the mighty Iroquois and the Conestoga, and in the southern states were the Choctaw, the Cherokee, the Creek, the Shawnee and many others comprising most of the major language family known as Algonquin. The vast open prairie land to the west which covered most of central America was the home of the Plains Indians, who made up the Siouan group and consisted finally of a number of tribes who did not populate this area until some 400 years ago. During the sixteenth century the Conquistadors brought horses to New Mexico. Tribe after tribe of Indians stole horses from the Spaniards or got them honestly by trading, then moved into the rich prairie land from all directions. The Sioux and Cheyenne came in from the east, Blackfoot from the north, Ute from the west and Pawnee and Comanche from the south. Arizona and New Mexico in the south-west contained Indians who were primarily village dwellers. These villages grew up quickly; the growing of corn became important, and the south-western culture was essentially peaceful and democratic. After the agriculturalists were driven out by more warlike tribes this became the land of the Pueblo Indians, the Zuni, the Hopi, the Pima, Mohave and Yuma. The Indians of the south-west included the Navaho and Apache, who were the wanderers, and probably the most recent arrivals in this area.

The great region comprising California and stretching north to include southern Alaska was the home of another group, the culture of which competes with that of the Arctic

*One of the Virginian
Indians painted by
John White in 1585,
when he accompanied
Ralegh on his first
colonizing expedition
to that region*

for the status of being the most distinctive and at the same time the most foreign in North America. Here lived the Tlingit of Alaska, the Tsimshian, Haida, Kwakiutl and Nookta of Canada, and the Chinook, Makah and Puget Sound tribes of Oregon and Washington. The last major culture area is contained in the great northern Arctic belt which stretches from Greenland to the Yukon, including 15,000 miles of coastline and embracing most of Canada and Alaska. This was the land of the Eskimo, a hardy people subsisting on the barest of necessities and forced to an existence of improvisation, who developed a culture which mainly depended on fishing and the hunting of the now much reduced caribou, seal and whales.

The hundreds of named tribes that make up the great Indian nation, with their widely differing customs and ways of life, have provided unlimited material for research and study by archaeologists, ethnographers, scientists and historians. The complete history of the American Indian has yet to be written, and to endeavour to search out a sequence applicable to the history of archery in war would be a task both unnecessarily complicated and inappropriate for our purpose. It is fairly safe to say, however, that every Indian tribe had the bow in one form or another, and that their use of the weapon varied according to custom, preference and geographical environment. Tribes of some areas also used other weapons which almost excluded the bow, such as the spear (often used with the *atl-atl*, or spear-thrower of the Aztecs), the club, possibly the oldest of weapons, and the sling, bolas and blowpipe.

The bow made of a single piece of wood, called the self-bow, was used wherever archery was known except in the central and eastern Arctic. In addition various types of sinew-backed bows were used and although the variants were governed by the raw materials readily available, they were usually developed to meet the particular needs of the area in which they were used. The general type of backing used by Indians living on the north Pacific coast, the western plains, California and as far down as the Mexican border, was made by gluing individual thread-like sinew fibres onto the back of the bow. Another principal form, used by Eskimos and some of their immediate neighbours as well as a few tribes in the south-west, is known as loose-backing, where braided or twisted sinew cords were laced back and

North American Indians of the seventeenth century, as faithfully recorded by de Bry. The proportions and form of the bows and arrows appear accurate; only the quivers are suspect

forth on the back of the bow-stave to give it extra strength.

At the time of the European contact, in 1492, the bow, in one form or another, was nearly universal in North America. Surprisingly enough the fiercely aggressive Aztecs, with their highly organized warrior society, hardly used the bow. The principal weapon of their armies was the *atl-atl*, which launched a feathered spear, in effect a large arrow. This was also true of some tribes further south, including the Incas of Peru and others who undoubtedly met the bow and arrow in opposition.

Beginning with the first voyage of Ponce de León to Florida in 1513, sixteenth-century historical and descriptive material on the Indians of the south-east is continuous and more abundant than for any other portion of America. By the time de León visited Florida, the bow had displaced the spear, which had been the principal weapon up to the beginning of the fifteenth century. The Indians who greeted de León and Hernandez de Cordoba, another Spanish navigator and adventurer, were probably the Calusa, who occupied the southern part of the Florida peninsula. Of powerful physique, the warlike Calusa were the fiercest fighters of the New World. Without preliminary palaver,

171

these natives fell upon all Spanish ships which visited the peninsula so fiercely that no permanent landings could be made for many years. They drove back all European attempts to enter their country, until eventually their numbers were greatly reduced by the introduction of European epidemic diseases. Before the end of the eighteenth century they had virtually ceased to exist as a tribe.

There is no question that the archery of the Indians of Florida made a deep impression on the Europeans who saw the power of this weapon at first hand. John Hawkins, who visited the area in 1565, particularly noted that 'In their warres they use bowes and arrowes', and another explorer to this area, wishing to test the power of native archery, offered a young Indian captive his liberty if he could shoot through a coat of mail. The garment was hung on a wicker basket and the Indian, standing 150 paces distant, shot a flint-headed reed through the armour. A second coat of mail was put over the first, and the Indian shot an arrow with great force through both. After this the Spaniards held their armour in contempt and devised a protection of felt or padded cloth which shielded them and their horses much better than chain or steel corselets. Some of the situations in which the early colonists found themselves were grim, especially when they were faced by muscular Indians armed with bows and arrows, and the many personal experiences recorded by these adventurers are punctuated with hair-raising incidents such as those which befell John Nicol and sixty-six other Englishmen in the Caribbean during the early seventeenth century. 'All this time neither Harry, Peter Stokesley's man, nor myself was shot; but as we thought desperately to burst through them into the narrow path, there came an arrow and pierced quite through his head, of which he fell suddenly, and I ran to lift him up, but he was dead without speaking one word to me at all. Then came there two arrows and hit me in the back, the one directly against my heart, the other through my shoulder blade. . . .' Nicol then ran into a group of Indians and found one of them '. . . with an arrow in his bow drawn against me, who stood until I came very near to him, for he purposed to have sped me with that shot, which when I espied it coming, I thought to have put it by with my sword, but, lighting upon my hand, it passed through the handle of my weapon, and nailed both together. Neverthe-

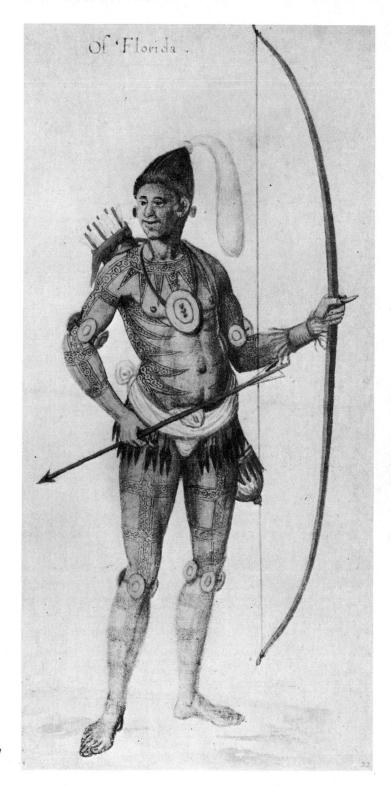

Of 'Florida.

Another of John White's drawings of the sixteenth century, showing an Indian from Florida with a powerful self-bow and business-like arrows

less I continued running at him still and before he could nock another, made him and all the rest turn their backs and flee into the sands again... '

Another series of colonizing expeditions to America was undertaken by Sir Walter Ralegh during the reign of the first Elizabeth. In 1585 John White, an illustrator of great charm and exceptional ability, accompanied Ralegh to Virginia, and the delightful watercolours which he produced have fortunately survived in excellent condition. His painting of an Indian warrior splendidly arrayed in full battle attire reveals much of interest. The half-naked and painted Virginian wears a fringed apron-like breech-cloth of leather and carries a longbow a little taller than himself. If the shrewd eye of John White enabled the bow to be correctly depicted, it would be from five feet nine inches to six feet, a self-bow, and almost identical in pattern to an English longbow. Arrows are carried in a tubular quiver slung at the bowman's waist and he wears a leather bracer on his left wrist. Another sixteenth-century work of considerable interest is *The History of America* by Theodor de Bry. In it can be found drawings of the Indians fighting the Spanish invaders and, although the musket is shown as the principal weapon opposing the Indians, the bow can be seen well in evidence, being used by both sides in the conflict.

The Delaware Indians, who occupied a region which included the land on which New York City now stands, were dressed similarly to the tribes further south and they, too, carried six-foot bows together with quivers containing flint-, bone- or antler-tipped arrows, and the fearsome war club of carved wood, with a ball-shaped head set at right angles from the handle, which became the popularly used tomahawk of later centuries.

The Indians of the south-east killed deer and other game with the bow and arrow and often hunted in large companies, as the bones of various animals, so common on their old kitchen refuse heaps, clearly prove. Together with the waging of war, hunting was the duty of the men of the tribe. Among the exhibits in the American Museum of Natural History is one which excellently illustrates the effect of the use of the bow in Indian warfare. The skeletons of three Indian warriors were excavated at Burial Ridge, Staten Island, in 1895. In the first skeleton, it was found that two arrow points of antler and one of bone had pierced the body

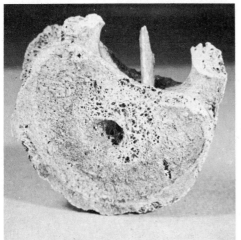
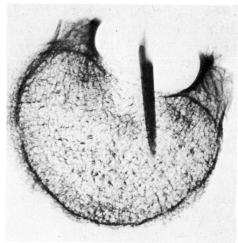

A human vertebra with the bone point of an arrow firmly embedded. The degree of penetration can be seen by the accompanying X-ray photograph

and lodged near the spinal column. Another point of argillite had been driven between two ribs, cutting a notch in each. Four more points of antler were found among the remains, but the most interesting wound of all was one where the antler-tipped arrow had ploughed through one side of the body and fully one-third of the point had passed through one of the ribs, making the hole in which it remained. The second warrior was also terribly injured. The left femur showed an elongated puncture near the lower end made by an arrow point. Among the ribs was the tip of an antler point, and another of yellow jasper was among the ribs on the left side of the body. Three other points were among the bones. The third skeleton likewise demonstrated the results of old-time bow play; twelve arrow-heads were found among its bones. The positions in which several of the points were found certainly speak well for the great force which propelled them; the longbows of the Indians must have been formidable weapons indeed. Taking into consideration the number of arrows that must have been embedded in the bodies of the warriors, it is probable that many of the projectiles were driven into the victims at close range after wounding.

The Iroquois tribes, close to the Great Lakes, were among the first to receive firearms from the early settlers, and on this account they soon abandoned the bow and arrow which, by 1727, had been entirely laid aside. But the gun did not replace the bow so quickly in most of the rest of North America, particularly further westward, to the

175

heart of the continent, where much of the history of American colonization was written.

The Plains, between the slopes of the Rocky Mountains on the west and the twenty-inch rainfall line on the east, and stretching from north of the Canadian border down almost to the Rio Grande in western Texas, was one of the greatest grazing areas the world ever knew. The land at first defied farming and it was not inviting to people without horses or metal, but it was the home of the buffalo, which ran wild on a scale almost beyond belief. With such a food supply there were bound to be communities of human beings, but the area was only very sparsely occupied. The Spanish explorers of 1540 and after spoke of the Indians who lived there in skin tents, who used dogs as beasts of burden, and hunted. They saw one Indian put an arrow through a buffalo, and remarked that this exhibition of primitive marksmanship would have been good work even with a musket. The horses that the Spanish brought into New Mexico ran wild and spread eastwards. From northern outposts in California, too, horses escaped and multiplied in Oregon. Rapidly the increasing equine population was captured and trained by the Indians of the north-west and traded to the east; and in the eighteenth century, one by one, the tribes surrounding the buffalo country learned to ride. Several major groups of Indians concerned with warfare among themselves pushed eastwards. The Sioux and the Cheyenne, all by now mounted, abandoned their farms and moved west. The Blackfoot, Crow and Comanche all turned to the new life, centred on the buffalo, which the domestication of the horse now made possible. By 1800 the cultural revolution was in full flower; the Indians had settled into a new way of life, and were now ripe for the greatest revolution of all, the coming of the white man. Throughout the whole of these vast upheavals the warriors and hunters of North America had carried bows and arrows which had remained unchanged. Apart from the use of new materials such as iron and bottle-glass for arrow-heads, the traditional form and construction had been maintained.

The Indians of the Plains possibly contributed most to the history of the United States in the mid-nineteenth century, and it was the tribes of this huge area of open prairie which came under the greatest scrutiny by pioneer travellers, explorers, military reporters, amateur ethnographers and scholars and artists attached to officially sponsored missions. Whereas it was from the early colonists and adventurers that we drew our knowledge of the Indians of the eastern woodlands, it is from the robust and colourful pioneers of the nineteenth century that we can assemble a picture of the Indian archers of the Plains. The tendency of many of these characters, however, was to exaggerate their accounts of the Indians' prowess and accuracy with the bow, and it is for this reason that such tales should be regarded with a certain amount of caution.

The composite tribes that made up the Plains Indians could not have survived without external enemies against whom their warrior associations could unite. These military societies were unique, and in many ways resembled the duelling societies of German students. A youth was permitted to join if he could demonstrate his courage, and the braver the warrior the higher would be his rank and status within these élite groups. Different tribes had differing rules and organizations, but in general these sodalities brought unity to a very diverse collection of peoples. Warfare became as ritualized as medieval knighthood, and it was only towards the end of the Plains culture that large battles took place in which Indian fought Indian or Indians fought the United States Army, with each group seeking to exterminate the other. Previous to that tactics consisted of forays and raids by small parties; the conflicts were brief and usually indecisive. The reason for the earlier form of aggression is that war was regarded as a game in which the players might win status by achievements graded according to the element of danger involved.

Tensions between the Indians and the Whites grew as the tide of settlers streamed westwards. Treaty after treaty was broken as Indian lands were sequestered by easterners covetous of acreage and precious metals. Soon the official policy became war of extermination. General Sherman, to his everlasting shame, said in 1867, 'The more I see of these Indians the more convinced I am that they all have to be killed or be maintained as a species of paupers.' The whole story is a tragic one of ham-fisted administration by the authorities, an almost complete absence of sympathetic diplomacy, and an appalling lack of understanding of Indian culture. No wonder, then, that the Indians believed they had been betrayed by the government in Washington;

177

from 1820 to 1890 they went on the war-path and the United States had an Indian problem. Raids on settlements and stagecoach routes reached such proportions that Washington had to send troops to protect them and to fight the Indians, who were often called the most formidable savage warriors ever encountered by white man.

Although the Indians' lack of numbers made it impossible for them to engage in disciplined assaults they developed the art of guerrilla warfare to a very remarkable degree, using stealth and cunning to make up for their deficiency in manpower. Their instinctive talents as hunters were now turned to the even more vital matter of self-preservation and, although their bows were supplemented by illegally obtained firearms, the bow and arrow remained the predominant weapon in early warfare. The use of the bow rather than the gun had the irreplaceable advantage of silence and, another vitally important consideration, there was no shortage of ammunition. 'We could not even distinguish the officer from his men. Each body was pierced by from twenty to fifty arrows, and the arrows were found as the savage demons had left them, bristling in the bodies.' So reported General George Armstrong Custer, a famous name in the history of Indian warfare, who, in a short time, mastered the battle tactics of the Indians as had few other regular officers of the United States Army. His memoirs contain many vivid eye-witness accounts of the conflicts between his troops and the Cheyenne, the Sioux and the Delaware Indians.

On one occasion Custer and his men were surprised at dawn, and his description of the initial attack by the Indians is a classic example of on-the-spot reporting: ' "O Heavens, General, look at the Indians!" Well might he (the guide) be excited. From every direction they dashed towards the band. Over the hills, from the west and the north, along the river, on the opposite bank, everywhere and in every direction they made their appearance. Finely mounted in full war paint, their long scalp locks braided with eagles' feathers, and with the paraphernalia of a barbarous war party—with wild whoops and exultant shouts, on they came ... a number of young Indian boys from fifteen to eighteen years of age crawled up and shot about fifty arrows into the circle in which the scouts lay. One of these arrows struck one of the men, Frank Herrington, full in the forehead. Not

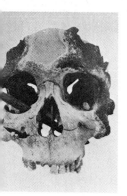

An Indian skull found in the San Joaquin valley, with a portion of an arrow shaft, probably originally equipped with a stone point, still in position. A full medical description and a reconstruction of the fatal event has been written by Saxton T. Pope

being able to pull it out, one of his companions, lying in the same hole with him, cut off the arrow with a knife, leaving the iron arrow-head sticking in his frontal bone; in a moment a bullet struck him in the side of the head, glancing across his forehead, impinged upon the arrow-head, and the two fastened together fell to the ground—a queer but successful piece of amateur surgery. Herrington wrapped a cloth around his head, which bled profusely, and continued fighting as if nothing had happened.' On another occasion, while engaged in rescuing two white girls, Custer and his men confronted a group of Indians without a shot being fired. A tense situation developed which could have exploded into a bloody incident if one false move had been made or one indiscreet word uttered. Custer admitted that he could recall no other experience with the Indians so exciting. 'Near me stood a tall, grey-haired chief, who, while entreating his people to be discreet, kept his cocked revolver in his hand ready for use, should the emergency demand it. He was one of the few men whom I had determined to hold. Near him stood another, a most powerful and forbidding looking warrior, who was without firearms, but who was armed with a bow, already strung, and a quiver full of iron-pointed arrows. He stood apparently unaffected by the excitement about him, but not unmindful of the surrounding danger. Holding the bow in one hand, with the other he continued to draw from his quiver arrow after arrow. Each one he would examine as coolly as if he expected to engage in target practice. First he would cast his eye along the shaft of the arrow, to see if it was perfectly straight and true. Then he would with thumb and finger gently feel the point and edge of the barbed head, returning to the quiver each one whose condition did not satisfy him. In this manner he continued until he had selected perhaps half-a-dozen arrows, with which he seemed satisfied, and which he retained in his hand, while his quick eye did not permit a single incident about him to escape unnoticed.' A tense situation indeed; but, happily, the girls were rescued without bloodshed.

One of the most fascinating, albeit gruesome, studies undertaken during the Indian troubles was a report by a United States Army surgeon of 1862, describing arrow wounds and their treatment in the field. 'The feathered end of the shaft protruding from the subject usually indicates

179

the diagnosis,' a premise which, although somewhat naïve, was a reminder that in the case of arrow-heads becoming detached, by accidental breaking away of the shaft or by design, as in the rankling type of arrow-head, past knowledge considered such wounds were beyond hope. In the old days extensive surgical search for an arrow-head embedded more than two and a half inches deep was not often carried out, and the arrow-head was left *in situ*, causing suppuration and death. Dr. Bill, of the U.S. Army, made some progress, and he improved on the earlier hit-and-miss methods, even designing special forceps for grasping and withdrawal of deeply embedded arrow-heads. One well-tried remedial measure, known and used since the fourteenth century, was recommended by Dr. Bill for certain wounds. This consisted simply of pushing arrow, arrow-head and all, forward to emergence rather than pulling it out. The sum total of experience of treatment of arrow wounds up to the mid-nineteenth century seems to be, 'Find out exactly how deep the arrow-head is embedded, preferably by touch. Pull it out, taking care not to detach the head from the shaft in the process, using forceps or other instruments, even kneeling on the patient to give added purchase. Or push the arrow through.' No mention was made of the use of anaesthesia, still in its infancy, and the cruder administration of ether or chloroform could only have slightly improved the victim's chances of survival.

Writing at the end of the eighteenth century, an early traveller described the results of Apache bowmanship, which nearly parallels the best penetration of the medieval longbow of England. 'The Apaches are incomparable archers, and seldom miss; their arrows, when let fly by a strong arm, have more power and effectiveness than a bullet from the best musket. As a proof, I wish to cite only one example, to which I myself was a witness. A mounted soldier was dispatched by his captain with letters to the captain of another garrison. His cloak, tightly folded by lengthwise, lay before him on the saddle and fell down part way over his left leg. Covering the cloak and the same leg hung his shield, made of three-ply, very thick oxhide, which hung down a little over the horse's belly. The soldier rode past a mountain where some Apaches lay in ambush and was stuck by one of their arrows, which passed through the shield, through the many folds of the folded cloak, through

180

the leg of the soldier, finally through the leather cover, and penetrated almost a quarter of an ell deep into the body of the horse. A bullet would scarcely have such force. When the soldier, fortunately saved by his swift mount, arrived at the place where I then was, I myself saw with amazement what had happened.'

The Apaches were typical of the Plains Indians, and their archery equipment was of a high standard of manufacture and finish; their arrows were especially well made. Their excellence was primarily due to the fact that the main part of the shaft was made of the reed called in the Apache language *klo-ka*, or 'arrow grass', which needs no straightening, whereas those arrows made by other tribes in the locality had to be straightened by a process that involved much labour and loss of time. Every Apache kept in the roof of his *jacal* a collection of these reeds to dry for making arrows, together with an extra mulberry bow. Although the Apaches generally used barbs of obsidian, which could be made in five to eight minutes, or of sheet iron, they also made them simply of triangular pieces of hard wood, in all respects resembling those first seen by Columbus upon reaching the continent.

Whereas the Indians of the eastern woodlands used self-wood bows, those from the western Plains and Sierra Nevada region of the west used bows of ash, mulberry, osage orange, yew, cedar and other woods, reinforced with animal sinew. This improvement consisted of a layer of shredded sinew, often chewed by the womenfolk to soften it, carefully arranged and glued to the back—the convex face—of the bow. Occasionally the long fibres of animal sinew would be additionally secured with a series of cross-lashings. Shorter and more powerful bows were the result. Another type of bow, found among the Sioux, can be described as a compound bow. It consists of several pieces of cow horn, mountain sheep horn or elk antler fitted together in a shape recalling the conventional 'Cupid' bow of artists. The sinew-backed bow, a short hard-hitting weapon easily managed from horseback, was ideal for the buffalo-hunting which occupied much of the time of the Plains Indians for the two centuries or so following the introduction of horses.

An examination of the dorsal vertebra of a buffalo that had been struck by an iron arrow-point reveals that there

181

was enough force to drive the arrow through the thick hide covered with matted woolly hair, several inches of flesh, through half an inch of solid bone, and to protrude, beyond the bone, more than half this distance again. This was the concentrated power, unleashed from the short bow of the mounted Indian, which brought the huge bulk of the buffalo to its knees. Further evidence of the penetrative force of Indian arrows is not lacking; stories of arrows piercing pine trees to a depth of six inches, of men being penetrated at 300 yards, of shafts sunk up to the feathers in the giant cactus in Arizona, even of headless arrows mortally wounding Government soldiers—these and other awesome and equally romantic tales can be quoted to compare the power of the bow with other primitive missile weapons.

'A Comanche on his feet is out of his element and comparatively almost awkward,' said Catlin, 'but the moment he lays hand upon his horse he gracefully flies away like an entirely different being.' Among the most impressive feats of horsemanship practised by this tribe, as well as by the Pawnees further west, was their way of throwing themselves down on the side of their horses while riding at full speed in the heat of battle. This effectively screened the rider from the enemy's weapons and in this position he was able to use his bow or lance in attack. 'This is a stratagem of war learnt and practised by every young man in the tribe,' continued Catlin, who observed that other tribes practised this feat but none could match the Comanche warriors. Some experts were able to perform the remarkable feat of shooting arrows under a horse's belly to deadly effect.

Catlin's notes, made while he was with the Blackfoot and Crows, give a description of the weapon used by them. 'The bow with which they are armed is small and apparently an insignificant weapon, though one of almost incredible power in the hands of its owner, whose sinews have been from childhood habituated to its use,' he wrote. 'The length of these bows is generally about three feet and sometimes not more than two and a half. They have no doubt studied to get the requisite power in the smallest compass possible, as it is more easily used on horseback than one of greater length. The greater part of these bows are made of ash and lined on the back with layers of buffalo or deer sinews to give greater elasticity. There are many also (amongst the Blackfoot and Crows) which are made of bone, and others of the horn of the mountain sheep. Those made from bone are decidedly the most valuable and cannot be procured short of the price of one or two horses ... and their arrows are headed with flint or bone, of their own construction, or with steel, as they are now chiefly furnished by the Fur Traders. The quiver which is uniformly carried on the back and made of the panther or otter skin, is a magazine of these deadly weapons, and generally carries two varieties. The one to be drawn upon a human enemy, generally poisoned and with long barbs designed to hang in the wound after the shaft is withdrawn, in which they are but slightly glued; and the other is used for their game, with the blade firmly fastened to the shaft and with the barbs inverted, that it may easily be drawn from the wound and used again.'

The use of the bow was part of the education of a boy; he was trained in archery from infancy and while still young was taught to make the best bow he could. Boys were often called out to shoot for prizes, and a great part of their leisure was taken up with constant target practice and fighting sham battles, which were spirited imitations of the successes of their elders. A favourite competition for the menfolk was the Game of Arrows. In this each contestant would add his wager to a winner-take-all prize. One by one each man would shoot his arrows into the air, endeavouring to see who could put the largest number in the air before the first struck the ground. Frequently as many as eight were put up before the first one fell. During the 1840s the United States Exploring Expedition witnessed Indian boys exercising with the bow; an extract from the official report read: 'They obtained an exhibition of the archery of the Indians by putting up a button at twenty yards [more probably feet] distance, which one of them hit three times out of five; the successful marksman was rewarded with it and a small piece of tobacco.' In addition to the use of the bow for hunting, the finding of arrow-heads embedded in human bones and occasional evidence of mass burials are ample indications that life was not entirely peaceful in the early south-west.

Warfare among the Hupa, from north-western California, consisted largely of feuds between their own kin groups or with corresponding groups in neighbouring tribes. The principal weapon was the bow and arrow. These were carefully and skilfully made, and the finest were produced by specialists who took great pride in their work and

183

A Navaho Indian using a short, sinew-backed bow to discharge stone-tipped arrows. Note the supply of arrows retained in the left hand ready for immediate use, a practice commonly found among primitive people

sold their products for a good price. The points of war arrows were not poisoned, but stone from certain places was regarded as particularly deadly. A special variety of flint obtained from a quarry on Mad River was considered 'deadly poison' and 'broke off in a wound, making it in-flamed'. This flint was never used on hunting arrows because it was 'too powerful'. Arrow-points were given supernatural power through special treatment and the reci-tation of magical formulas, and feathers from a small kind of hawk were believed to make arrows more accurate. Bows and arrows were strictly cared for and, when not in use, were carried in skin bow-cases slung under the left arm. These cases were stuffed with moss to serve as a cushion for the arrow-points.

Cunning, treachery, ambushing and surprise attacks played an important part in Hupa warfare. Pitched battles occurred only when two enemy parties met face to face or when one was forewarned of an impending attack; once the fighting began, no order was observed and each man fought as he wished. A skilled fighter was able to dodge arrows either by watching his opponent's bow or the arrow itself. The ability to dodge flying missiles was developed from an early age, when rough boyhood games included duels in which the contestants threw oak balls, bits of wood or other objects at each other. It is said that a good warrior watched an enemy's bow, observing which end moved, because the arrow was thrown in that direction, and he might then dodge the opposite way. The arrow was observed in flight and, if not aimed directly at a man, it could be seen in the sunlight and avoided. Womenfolk sometimes joined in the fight with clubs and stones, and both women and children ran about picking up arrows. The duration of the conflict was fairly short and, as Hupa weapons were not particularly deadly, casualties were few.

The aggressive use of the bow by North American Indians was secondary to its use as a weapon for survival. The skills developed for the latter, and most widespread, use provided the basic tactics for the former. Perhaps the most important factor in the evolution of the Indian warrior was the introduction of the horse, which also provided a new dimension for his hunting methods. But whereas the new-found mobility led to over-hunting of the buffalo for instance, and to that creature's virtual extinction, the same facility revolutionized warfare by giving the Indians the means to perform *blitzkrieg* tactics. The marriage of skilled horsemanship and expert archery was a combination difficult to contest. It was really only a matter of time, together with a preponderance of well-fed soldiers with superior fire-power, and not a little intrigue and unfair state-craft, that finally crushed the Indians. It was only the late arrival of the gun that finally replaced the bow and arrow as the universal weapon of the Red Indian and reduced it to a curiosity to be collected as a tourist trophy.

CHAPTER 10

War among savages

In the eighteenth century it was assumed that the primitive state of mankind was one of Arcadian peace, joy and contentment. In the nineteenth century the assumption went over to the other extreme—that the primitive state was one of universal warfare. This, like the former notion, is a great exaggeration. Man in the most primitive and uncivilized state known to us does not practise war all the time; he dreads it. He might rather be described as a peaceful animal. Real warfare comes with the collision between more developed societies, and the aggressive nature of primitive man is largely aggravated by confrontation with those societies who call themselves civilized. The way in which the indigenous peoples of North America responded to the rape of their lands by whites is a familiar pattern that has been repeated in other parts of the world where primitive cultures remained relatively unchanged into modern times.

Most of these primitive tribes lived by hunting, and the predominant weapon found among them is the bow and arrow. When the occasion demanded, the skills necessary for hunting were adapted for aggression against man. As a rule this aptitude for war among primitive peoples is the result of necessity—to prevent extinction or enslavement—and it follows that the more primitive groups became involved in hostilities, the better they became at using bows and arrows as warlike weapons. The use of incendiary arrows is a clear example of such adaption. Such a device would be completely useless when hunting animals, as the sight of a flaming missile would act as an early warning of

Veddahs, aboriginal people of Ceylon, armed with their simple, self-wood bows and bamboo-tipped arrows. From a nineteenth-century photograph

danger and scare off such game, whereas in offensive situations literally 'smoking out' the enemy is a ruse not without tactical advantage. It was not only the personal safety of families and tribal groups and their possessions that was at risk, it was also the traditional culture of these groups, and the better primitive man was able to defend himself, the more chance there was of retaining the identity of tribes whose life-styles had survived for many centuries.

Other than defensive warfare, caused by threats from foreign invasion, the hostilities that occur domestically among primitive peoples are rarely more than feuds, quarrels or disagreements which erupt into personal combat between individual offenders; group or tribal conflict, usually short lived and decided by a point of honour; or mock battles which, none the less, can be dangerous to life and limb. To generalize on the warlike nature or otherwise of those peoples we like to classify as primitive is impossible, and we can only refer to some groups who have demonstrated their aptitude in aggressive or defensive involvements and particularly their use of bows and arrows in such situations.

During the late nineteenth century there were scores of colourful characters who explored the hitherto dangerous and unknown areas of the primitive world. Most appeared to have stepped out of the pages of fiction, and their exploits were as extreme as their personalities. A typical example was George E. Morrison, who, at the age of nineteen, shipped as an apprentice surgeon in the Pacific, walked for 2,043 miles across Australia in 123 days, and at the age of twenty-one set off for New Guinea with an ill-assorted group of companions. 'The men I did engage,' he wrote later, 'were with one exception, curious customers.' These were Ned Snow, 'remarkably short and of such eccentric conformation that, whereas his body seemed longer than his legs, his head appeared more lengthy than either', a Malay named Cheerful, 'who subsequently proved to be an opium smoker and an incarnate devil', a New Hebridian named Lively; the exception was John Lyons, 'a tall athletic young fellow of excellent character, a good bushman and excellent prospector'.

Morrison's trip to New Guinea was disastrous. Various misfortunes overtook him and his team, and the venture culminated in an attack by tribesmen armed with bows and arrows. Two arrows hit Morrison without warning. 'One of them penetrated my stomach just under the chest, and the other entered the hollow of my right eye and stuck in the bone at the bottom of the bridge of my nose.' Morrison fell to the ground, pulled out the arrow from his eye, and snapped off the shaft protruding from his stomach. Other arrows were shot at him, but he managed to escape with the help of two of his companions and suffered an agonizing journey of thirteen days back to Port Moresby.

Eventually he reached hospital with half his face paralysed and the loss of use of one leg. One arrow-head of bamboo was removed from the back of his throat and the second, which the surgeons of Melbourne had considered too deep for safe operation, was eventually removed at Edinburgh University. Morrison recovered enough to qualify in medicine and surgery and set off again on his travels, which took him halfway round the world, and in 1893 he journeyed from Shanghai to Rangoon wearing Chinese clothes and a false pigtail.

A number of other intrepid explorers, prospectors and hunters, all having somewhat eccentric and almost theatrical qualities, recorded their adventures and exploits in the Pacific, and the tribe that attacked Morrison, first officially noticed as late as 1899, is mentioned often in these accounts. It is the Kukukuku, 'little bowmen with cloaks of beaten bark and girdles of human thigh bones', who inhabited the interior of New Guinea. It was said of this tribe that 'the bow usually opens hostilities and a stone-headed club concludes them'. In open fighting the Kukukukus usually lobbed flights of arrows onto the enemy, moving through the high grass in open formation. Spotters on the flanks often directed the aim by shouted signals. Stealthy raiding by small bands was the preferred method of warfare, however, and these tribesmen depended more on ambush and on surprise than on good shooting. Speed in shooting was no doubt valuable, especially in close-range skirmishes.

Well into this century Kukukuku men and boys spent most of their time in the village making bows and arrows: 'Each makes his own, to the length that suits him.' While war arrows are plain compared with those made for hunting and other purposes, care was taken to match them in sets for constant flight. The plain, unbarbed arrows rarely killed a man in a fight. Gold prospector Arthur Darling survived

Kukukuku tribesman from the Eastern Highlands, New Guinea

189

five arrows when the Kukukuku attacked him in 1910, and another prospector named Frank Pryke was twice attacked by the Kukukukus after provoking them, and on the second occasion 'an arrow went very nearly through his body, and would probably have killed anyone else. Mr. Pryke, however,' wrote Judge Murray, 'simply pulled it out and went on prospecting.' Pryke published a collection of poems, and had his own comments about these primitive warriors:

> We know the Kukukuku well
> And have met their warriors bold
> Of many startling things could tell
> When we searched their land for gold
> If near their village meeting
> We would with them try to trade
> They would return no friendly greeting
> To the advances which we made
> Followed by an arrow flight
> 'Ere we'd even got a notion
> That they intended fight...

The story is a familiar one; invasion by strange white men into the homeland of simple people whose natural instinct is to defend themselves—often misinterpreted as aggression. Morrison, Pryke and Darling were lucky, and lived; many other adventurers were killed by the long, bamboo-bladed arrows of other tribesmen from the highlands of New Guinea. The arrow-heads look deceptively simple—leaf-shaped slivers cut from bamboo stems, possessing razor-sharp cutting edges, designed to be used against tough-skinned beasts and ideally suited for their dual rôle against human targets. Their bows, too, were uncomplicated, being self-bows of some tough and flexible wood of the palm family—similar in size and design to the early longbows of Europe, but cruder—or thick and long bamboo bows. Apart from the bamboo-headed shafts, the range of arrows included some with long hardwood foreshafts, some sharpened to spikes and others fashioned into vicious barbs and serrations, with tips carefully under-cut to break off in a wound. There were, in addition, arrows provided with points made from such items as the spines of the sting-ray, cassowarys' claws and splinters of bones from small game.

In recent years considerable interest has been shown in

190

the tribes of New Guinea, and they have been the subject of numerous studies as a surviving 'Stone Age' culture. Until a few years ago the tribes of the central mountain valleys went to war with bows and arrows and shields decorated with abstract geometrical motifs. The shields, made of flat planks about an inch thick, as tall as a man's eye level, were carried by a bearer who gave protection to himself and one or two archers. The Tipalmin, of the upper Ilam valley, believe that the shields possess a spirit and they treat them as sentient beings. They give them names and tell them when a battle is about to begin. In response the shields give out a low drumming noise at the approach of fighting, make themselves light when carried into battle, and swell when an arrow strikes them so as to stop it bursting through. Fighting took place either by ambushes mounted by small raiding parties or in more formal battles. In a fight the acknowledged experts carried only three arrows and shot deliberately at individuals, rarely missing, while the rank and file carried a great bunch of arrows and let fly as fast as they could shoot, filling the air with clouds of arrows. The enemy dead were eaten, regardless of age or sex, and the undergrowth was beaten to flush out any people who had escaped. Some men were so adept at dodging, even when faced with close-range shooting, that they never used shields—a risky business, nevertheless, when one is attacked by weapons so powerful that shots right through a man were commonplace.

Any reference to the 'South Seas' immediately conjures up romantic notions of tropical islands with palm-lined bays, populated by tribes of cannibals and nubile maidens clearing away the remains of half-digested missionaries. Many of these stories were brought back by centuries of travellers, explorers and missionaries and, if one allows for over-enthusiastic reporting, the descriptions of these visits provide a vivid picture of the sort of reception foreigners could expect.

The exploration of the Pacific by Europeans was begun, mainly by the Spanish from America, in the sixteenth century; but the true discoverers were those who first populated the islands centuries earlier. The first European visitors to New Guinea seem to have been the Portuguese in 1511. The Solomon Islands were discovered in 1568 by Mendaña, but were not seen again by Europeans for 200 years. Mendaña returned to the Pacific in 1595 and tried unsuccessfully to establish a colony on Santa Cruz.

Activity during the seventeenth century was mostly by the Dutch. In 1616 Le Maire and Schouten sailed along the north coast of New Guinea and discovered New Ireland and some of the small islands off the Solomons, and in 1643 Tasman sighted Fiji. The eighteenth century saw the great exploring voyages which mapped the Pacific, leaving only details for later comers to fill in. Carteret rediscovered the Solomons and the Santa Cruz group in 1767. In 1768 Bougainville revisited Espiritu Santo, and in 1770 Cook passed through the Torres Straits. Cook discovered and charted most of the remainder of the New Hebrides, and also first visited New Caledonia in 1774. In the following 100 years the map of Melanesia was completed by a multitude of explorers, surveyors, whalers, traders, labour recruiters and missionaries.

Mendaña, describing the natives of Santa Cruz in 1595, says they were armed with bows and arrows, some of the latter being pointed with bone and anointed with some poison, which the Spaniards, however, did not believe to be very deadly. On this and later occasions many of the European adventurers were wounded by arrows, but it is not known to what extent these wounds proved fatal. A great number of instances occur in early and later voyages, in which the natives succeeded in driving off unwelcome visitors by shooting volleys of their supposedly poisoned arrows at those who attempted to land.

The use of poison in this region is a subject that puzzled early travellers, because no firm conclusions could be arrived at concerning the composition of the poison or even as to whether deaths, when they occurred, were directly attributable to the toxic nature of the arrow-head, to the wound itself, or to the septicaemia or tetanus which frequently appeared to be the official cause of death. Although the conclusions of a Navy report of 1876 point to deliberate attempts by the natives to poison their arrows, there were no recorded instances that would prove without doubt that fatalities were directly caused by poisoned arrows. What was probable was that the substances that were smeared on arrow-points created irritation and inflammation and delayed healing of wounds, which, in turn, allowed other infection to occur.

Her Majesty's ship *Pearl* travelled to the South Seas in 1875, with a crew who were well aware of the results of the 'deadly flights of poisonous arrows', and were cautiously on guard against such an event. After safely passing through the New Hebrides group, landing and making excursions to collect material, the *Pearl* proceeded to the Santa Cruz Islands, where they met the resistance from the natives that they had feared who were, according to the official report, 'notorious for their obstinate resistance to the advances of missionaries, traders and white people under any guise'. In a 'treacherous and unprovoked attack' two or three officers and a handful of men were hit by arrows when trying to make a landing. One officer received a wound from an arrow held in the hand of an islander, which implies that arrows could double up as spears in close-quarter fighting.

The wounds were taken very seriously on account of the bad repute of the deadly nature of the arrow-heads, and a precise and detailed record of the treatment given to each sailor was kept. Two seamen and two officers survived and were returned to duty after a couple of weeks, but three seamen and the Commodore himself died in spasm eight days after being wounded. There is strong evidence to suggest that the demise of these men was partly due to fear and hysteria. The psychological aspects of the use of poisoned arrows are deep, and from this 100-year-old report it is clear that hysteria had developed from the fear of the unknown danger connected with poisoned arrows and the apprehension of a wound causing untold agonies. Deliberate or not, the effects of such psychological warfare have to be regarded as extremely effective. The traditional beliefs associated with the use of 'poisoned' arrows among the natives are strong enough to provide a substantial psychological weapon amongst these primitive people. In other parts of the world where poisoned arrows were used they seem generally to have been intended for hunting. The legendary curare of the Amazon, which has connotations of special mysteries, was considered unsuitable for use against humans as it was thought to be a cowardly method of killing men.

Sensational stories circulated freely concerning the gruesome processes involved in making native poisons. One story, typical of many, was related by an American in command of a small trading ship plying among the islands of

193

Polynesia, who said he saw one or two dead bodies lying in a state of decomposition, with several arrows sticking in them 'like porcupines, sir', while sitting by them was a native, with a wood fire and a pot of vegetable poison, who drew the arrows from the body dripping with viscid animal matter, held them over the fire until they were partially dry, then smeared them with the contents of the pot.

Such reports as these have been assembled partly from facts and partly from information collected by questioning the natives. For example, an islander who was asked how arrow points were made deadly, answered 'from dead men', from which incorrect conclusions resulted in artificially exaggerated reports. More accurate is the report by Codrington, of 1889, who carefully documented an account of the preparation of poisoned arrows on the island of Maevo, one of the New Hebrides group.

'First a skeleton was dug up, the long bones broken into splinters and cut into proper shape, before being finished by rubbing on coral rock with water. Then the bone was fixed into a tree-fern wood foreshaft, charms being sung or muttered the while. Next the juice of the *no-to* plant (*excoevaria agallocha*) was put on the bone and the head set aside in a cool, damp place where a substance like mould grew on it. The next step involved digging up the root of the *loko* creeper, cooking the inner fibre and squeezing it into the leaf of the nettle tree. With a piece of stick, this mixture was spread on the bone and the head put back in a cool, damp place, where the covering swelled up in lumps and then became smooth as it dried. At this stage, the head was inserted in the shaft, and the head painted over with a green earth found in only one spot on the island. After painting, the arrow was taken to the beach and dipped in seawater until the covering became hard.'

Maevo tradition ascribes the invention of this arrow to a blind man, Muesarava, his innovation being the use of human bone in place of animal and bird bone. Muesarava killed many of his enemies until, in answer to a question from the survivors, he revealed his secret and was soon afterwards killed by his own invention. The original piece of bone used by Muesarava was preserved until the last century, although the shaft had been replaced many times. These arrows were found all over the archipelago and were feared by native and European alike. Some old men, and women,

Fearsome warrior-hunters from New Guinea. Their long, bamboo-headed arrows often exceed the length of their bows

194

specialized in making the most effective poisoned arrows.

Arrows equipped with human bone points appear in other parts of this region, and such arrow-heads are thought to possess *mana*, the ghostly force or magic power of the dead man. A piece of such bone, broken off in an arrow wound, introduced tetanus bacillus, which, left to germinate in human tissue, produced virulent toxins. The native himself, when making these arrows, did not have the idea of killing with a specific poison. The active agent was the spiritual power or *mana* of the man who had been split up into arrow-heads. It was a magical process. He observed that a man so shot usually died, therefore the magic worked.

Warfare was endemic throughout Melanesia and still persists in a few places. Generally it was a matter of skirmishes arising from clan or village feuds, or of head-hunting raids carried out by small mobile parties. Ambushes and night attacks were favourite tactics; in battle most tribes carried extra arrows in bamboo tubes, apart from those normally carried in the hand, and frequently fought behind large hardwood shields, a unique and sophisticated innovation among primitive peoples. Sometimes, as in the New Hebrides, pitched battles were fought by arrangement on recognized fighting grounds. In some areas warfare on a larger scale was known; this was especially the case in Fiji, where parties of mercenaries from Tonga took service with Fijian chiefs. In most of the islands fighting would usually cease when one or two men had been killed or wounded. It was rare for a tribe to be annihilated or driven out of its territory in the course of a single campaign, but pressure by expanding groups and the consequent continual warfare undoubtedly caused considerable alteration and movement of populations.

The pursuit of war was not always a dominant factor among primitive peoples and this is the case when we consider the Indians of Brazil. The bow is as much a part of the lives of these Indians as any of their personal possessions and they rarely move anywhere outside the village without carrying bows and arrows, ready for immediate use. The use of archery in hostile situations can be generally described as a long-range weapon more often used to soften the enemy rather than to effect mass casualties. As a rule Brazilian Indians regarded the killing of their enemies by such a weapon as having lesser value than by dealing the

Inter-tribal conflict—a raiding party attacks a stockaded village in sixteenth-century Brazil

fatal blow at close quarters with a club. They regard killing beyond arm's length as somewhat insulting to victor and vanquished, and purposeful killing by means of shooting with arrows is often reserved for wrongdoers such as adulterers and inefficient sorcerers. Accounts of engagements between rival tribal groups are rare and it is not easy to form a general pattern of the warfare that occurs amongst these people.

The concept of aggression has special meanings among Brazilian Indians, and to create the right emotional conditions and to attract and store up the requisite magic power to ensure the success of a hostile enterprise, various formalities and ceremonial preparations have to be observed. For the Brazilian Indians, as in other primitive societies, to prepare for war it is necessary to put on war paint, to perform dance ceremonials and to abstain from intercourse prior to actual hostilities. Additionally, ceremonies of aggression are enacted in which initiated men ritually attack uninitiated boys, and the killings are mimed. This expression of bellicosity is often not confined to ritual situations, however, as the actors frequently become too realistically in-

197

volved in their parts. The bow and arrow plays an important part in these rituals; it is a symbol of aggression and death, and in actual war bows and arrows that had been used for killing humans were considered to be polluted and were discarded after use.

A modern study of one tribe from central Brazil, meticulously recorded by David Maybury-Lewis, includes a fascinating account of a conflict between rival groups which lasted five years. The detailed causes of this lengthy feud are complex. Briefly the whole matter was sparked off by the killing of a member of one tribe who, by his plotting and scheming, became a threat to the authority of the dominant factor of a rival group. A few members of each tribe in turn were ambushed and killed, the reprisals becoming more and more violent and leading to skirmishes and village raids. The situation rapidly deteriorated, and one group planned in earnest to mount a major offensive against those who had begun it all and who were feared as powerful sorcerers.

The attackers painted themselves for war and attacked at dawn. The action was well planned. They converged on the enemy village from three sides and approached so silently that even the dogs did not bark. They took the village completely by surprise, and as groups moved in they were covered by warriors with bows at the ready to pick off anyone who escaped. One arrow, well directed, silent and fatal, put an end to the curiosity of one defender, killed instantly when he came out to see what was happening. Many others tried to escape by plunging into the river that barred their egress on the fourth side. Some of the attackers lined the opposite river bank and picked off those in the water by precise arrow-shots.

Through the early morning there was parleying and desultory shooting of arrows, and eventually intermediaries managed to persuade the attackers to return home. The feud continued, however, and other groups were drawn in through lineage alliances and long-standing quarrels. Open warfare between the two rival factions now really began and once started it could not easily be stopped. There was no customary manner of bringing such hostilities to an end. Usually the minority groups in a community take the lead in calming the bellicosity of the majority. The form of warfare that began the conflict was the pattern which con-

Umotina warrior preparing to shoot, wearing a ceremonial shield of animal skins. From the Mato Grosso, Brazil

199

tinued, with slight variations, for the five years it lasted. This was a competition for the leadership rather than for the usual spoils of war, in which all adult men were involved, whether they liked it or not. Casualties were invariably light—otherwise the hostilities could not have continued for so long. Every villager was adept at shooting the bow, a very necessary skill, which was taught from very early childhood, and therefore each tribe had a full complement of potential warriors, all equally dextrous in the handling of bows and arrows. This probably accounts for the fact that there was little in the way of planned or organized battle situations; it was not necessary to train for war, as a call to arms was nothing less than another hunting party.

Depending on the motivation of a belligerent situation, Indians either mount a concerted expedition or organize small raiding parties. The latter situation is typical in regional hostility, where tribes or villages are engaged in permanent feuding or where they set out to capture prisoners or trophies for social prestige within their society.

In many cases, when war is intermittent, warnings are given for the opening of hostilities, and these signals may or may not be verbal. Arrows are often used as a warning sign, or as a declaration of war. When Indians observe the approach of other groups into their territory they place two crossed arrows in their path. This is a universally known sign. The Txikao use a more eloquent method of showing that they are hostile to strangers. Along the well-worn path to their village they dig a pit, at the bottom of which a group of spears are set up, and the hole is disguised with branches and leaves. A little further on they erect two small figures made of tree bark, painted and adorned with feathers. The purpose is to attract the attention of the invader so that, if he did not heed the warning, looking up, he would fall into the trap.

Once war is declared by such means, or at least sufficiently strong reasons are given for hostilities, the men are psychologically prepared to attack their neighbours, and the tactics then employed depend on the situation. Generally speaking the Indians avoid open battle and rely on ambush or tactical surprise. Night attacks on villages are preferred in which, apart from the use of incendiary arrows, the weapons generally used are the club and spear to attack the half-asleep and partially asphyxiated inhabitants who escape from their burning houses. A general tactic of attack is to approach close to the enemy village, and after the routines and habits of the people have been studied, to launch an assault. Where there are no alternatives, bows and arrows are used to soften the enemy in readiness for hand-to-hand combat, and we have many reports which indicate that this method predominates among Brazilian Indians. 'The attack generally began with arrows shot from ambush and this was followed by a dashing assault with clubs and lances,' and 'if the enemy barricaded themselves indoors ... the house was set on fire by their incendiary arrows', are typical observations by anthropologists who studied these remote tribes.

Nimuendaju, when he was engaged in pacifying one such tribe, built a house with an iron roof so that it could not be set on fire by incendiary arrows. The fall of the roof was such that it extended low over the verandah, which faced the forest. The occupants of the house, although protected from direct arrow-shots, could be seen by the Indians so that communication at a distance would be possible. The Indian attack began with arrows shot from the cover of the forest, and when they saw no counter-attack materialize they became more audacious, shooting clouds of arrows at the house and its inhabitants. Finally, aware of the pacific intentions of the white men, they abandoned their belligerency, thus opening the way to other, more peaceful forms of contact.

Reports of Indian tactics clearly indicate that the bow and arrow is the principal weapon used for attacks from a distance, and in such situations the blow-pipe is rarely used. It is interesting to note that the reasons given by the Indians for the choice of weapon are merely justifications, and the actual motivations more often than not follow patterns far deeper than practical considerations. For example, the Jivaro, who are expert users of the blow-pipe with poisoned darts, never use this weapon in war. According to them such use would render the weapon ineffective against animals, adding that in fighting men they prefer to inflict large wounds and shed as much blood as possible, difficult to achieve with small blow-pipe darts but relatively easy to achieve by means of long, razor-sharp blades of bamboo, shot with deadly accuracy into chest or neck and causing the maximum haemorrhage.

The intrusion of European culture in Africa accelerated the decline of the bow as a warlike weapon, which was already slowly being supplanted by the spear as the principal weapon among many tribes. The European contact in the fifteenth century brought with it changes in weapons and cultures and this, coupled with the fact that intricate immigration patterns overran much of the continent, leads to problems when one speaks of the indigenous population of Africa. To deal generally with the use of the bow as a weapon among so many different tribes presents many difficulties. By the end of the last century the bow ceased to exist in North Africa, and it is a historical fact that it was unknown in almost the whole territory of South-East Africa. Conversely, the bow was the only weapon in some areas, and between these two extremes there are many tribes who regarded the bow with varying importance. Among some tribes the full use of the bow as a primarily aggressive weapon has been superseded by its use as a weapon reserved for set-piece conflicts arranged to settle disputes and quarrels. Among Kung Bushmen of southern Africa, when men in an intermediate kinship group fight each other over some marital quarrel, sharing dispute, or mysterious sudden death that cannot be explained, they shoot at each other with poisoned arrows or hurl poisoned spears. They fight face to face, dodging the missiles, and do not shoot as accurately as they do when hunting, scoring frequent misses! Now and then bystanders are hit by mistake and killed, including women and boys. Their poison takes about six hours to kill a man, and when one is hit others may cut the wound to make it bleed, and try to suck the poison out, but still the wound is often fatal. The Pygmies also use poisoned arrows, principally for hunting, but when their enemies discover their hideouts and attack them, they climb trees and defend their positions by shooting at the intruders with their poisoned arrows. As with the Bushmen, the fighting habits of the Pygmies are locally variable and dependent on local circumstances.

Hordes of travellers, prospectors and scientists adventured into the jungles of the Dark Continent, inevitably to meet ineffectual, but none the less enthusiastic, opposition from the natives. This opposition, by warriors armed with—sometimes very puny—bows and arrows, 'cost the white colonizers many youthful lives'. The pattern varied from region to region, some tribes preferring to use the bow equally with the spear, others carrying the spear but discarding it in battle as a hindrance and using only the bow, and some spear warriors suddenly producing bows and arrows when faced with an aggressive situation. Possessing both weapons, some hunt and others use only spears. Insofar as the tribes of Africa are concerned, the use of the spear and bow as auxiliary weapons is an extremely interesting study, and notice must be taken of the two weapons as having interchanging and complementary rôles.

Other primitive peoples have used the bow in aggressive situations in ways very similar to the indigenous peoples of Africa, such as the now virtually extinct Andamanese, who were noted for settling grievances by sudden raids at dawn while everyone was asleep, or in the late afternoon when they were busy cooking and eating. The raiders either crept through the jungle or approached by canoes. They leapt on their victims by surprise, quickly shot all the men and women unable to escape, and took away uninjured children to adopt them. If enough members of the group survived to reconstitute the band, they might eventually grow numerous enough to seek revenge, and a lengthy feud could arise.

Apart from these full-scale feuds, when men of the same group became angry with each other, they berated their opponents and broke things to vent their anger. Now and then two men would shoot arrows at each other, usually aiming wide of the mark, and the rest of the people would disappear into the forest. If one man actually killed another, the murderer dashed out into the forest and stayed away for a few weeks until the others had simmered down. Staying out alone at night was punishment enough, because of the fear of jungle spirits and because of the special steps that had to be taken to keep his victim's ghost from harming him.

Perhaps the most sophisticated solution to the difficult situations of conflict that arise within primitive cultures occurs within the Ona of Tierra del Fuego. Main causes of conflict usually began with trespass in search of game. Such transgressions could grow into full-scale feuds which may be settled by war, in the form of raiding parties, a wrestling bout—in which contestants were replaced as they became exhausted—or, if neither recourse settled the matter, a chal-

*Oras Indian from
Tierra del Fuego, fully
armed for war with
his massive self-wood
bow and battle club*

lenge to single combat. The challenger appeared naked outside the enemy camp, and his enemy shot six arrows at him,
the challenger dodging and advancing with each step. If he
survived, the challenger shot at his enemy in a similar
fashion, or at a relative of the enemy if the latter was a poor
dodger. To retreat during this ordeal was a great disgrace.
In many cases one of the men was killed or wounded. When
peace was finally agreed the last strange, but logically
satisfying, act was performed. Each man on each side made
five headless arrows, but with a wrapped rawhide disc near
the point, intended to wound, but not to kill. Each man
gave his five arrows to his worst enemy, who then shot them

204

at him rapidly, whilst he ran towards the shooter. Thus most of the participants were wounded to some extent, and by their own arrows, and each man had a crack at his favourite antagonist. This painful, but non-lethal, performance terminated the feud.

The European contact with the primitive societies of three continents brought with it the trappings of civilization, including new diseases, guns, alcohol, labour kidnapping and cultural disintegration, and old ways of living were smothered by the demands of new societies. The skills of archery and the special arts of primitive warfare, with all the esoteric and practical accomplishments associated with bows and arrows, have been lost. Much of the natural environment of the indigenous peoples of the world remains; however, the pathetic few who still survive in these areas have, in many cases, lost their very *raison d'être*, and struggle to survive by making a few crude copies of bows and arrows to sell as tourist souvenirs. Their history is no less important than that of the Western World, and their future is in the hands of those who forced them to conform to the insatiable demands of a technologically based economy. The arguments for scientific advancement are strong, but it is a matter of conscience rather than progress that should determine the future of the sad remnants of once proud native peoples.

CHAPTER 11

The last of the Bowmen

Although archery as a predominant weapon of war suffered a decline in every area of the civilized world where it had previously flourished, its final demise was dictated by the eagerness with which new weapons were taken up and the extent to which the use of bows and arrows was tolerated. We have seen that during the Elizabethan era, for example, stalwarts who supported the retention of bows and arrows as official weapons were not easily silenced. From time to time this enthusiasm, for what had undoubtedly become an old-fashioned weapon, flared up, and in later centuries further attempts were made to reintroduce the bow. In addition some nations did not give up the bow as quickly as others, and here and there it remained an officially recognized military weapon even into the twentieth century. Other instances of the use of the bow in military situations occurred in isolation, usually promoted by individuals whose love of the bow found expression in times of national emergency.

There is a variety of instances in which the bow has been used aggressively in modern times. In many cases it is hardly surprising that archery as a weapon has continued, for example among native tribes, but in other areas it has occasionally featured very briefly among those peoples who have thought themselves more sophisticated in the choice of weapons. Isolated instances of encouragement for a wider use of the bow in modern warfare crop up now and again in recent history, and one consistent feature given in its favour is the element of surprise occasioned by its use in selected incidents. In operation its silence, or very nearly so, is unique among missile weapons and perhaps this, above anything else, has appealed to the military idealist. As a weapon that can be used effectively against individual targets, and that can cause fatalities instantly and silently, it has never been equalled.

In England during the seventeenth century it was to be expected that some attempts were made to retain the bow as an official weapon. Apart from its practical warlike application, two other advantages became apparent—it was cheap to produce in quantity compared with the early clumsy and expensive handguns, and it was simple to operate; a country peasant with only the minimum of training could quickly become reasonably proficient in its use.

The introduction of the use of gunpowder on a wide scale encouraged the writing of manuals on that subject, and at least two books, *The Gunner, showing the whole practice of Artillery*, and *The Art of Gunnery*, include instructions on the use of incendiary arrows to be shot from longbows, crossbows and handguns. One slim volume of 1628 was devoted entirely to the use of incendiary arrows. It was entitled *A New Invention of Shooting Fire-shafts in Long Bows*, in which the anonymous author describes practice with incendiary arrows shot from longbows at a tethered bull—'men might then make trial with their fire-shafts (a brave manly sport) where happly the madding of the enraged beast (besides inuring men to conflict) would teach some profitable strategems for war.' The author, 'a True Patriot', goes on to plead his case by claiming that 'no fairer engine was ever used in war, the cost not great, the incumbrance not at all: they are neat, portable, and so manageable, that even children make their sport with them, and youths of any growth may do good service, making their practice only with the common arrows.'

Frontispiece to A New Invention of Shooting Fire-Shafts in Long-Bowes, *published by 'A True Patriot' in 1628*

This was the age of impractical propositions and hare-brained schemes. William Neade had a plan for combining the bow with the pike, which resulted in a commission from Charles I for Neade and his son to teach the two weapons together. The suggestion was too late to be popular and undoubtedly too cumbersome to put into practice and, after attempts to set the scheme on a practical and an economic basis, nothing more is heard of the Neades and their unusual proposals.

Eminent military men, ministers and other influential persons put the case for the reintroduction of the bow into the trained bands and for the raising of archery companies. Sir James Turner in 1670 argued the case of the bow versus the musket and suggested that if a half or a third of the forces were archers much of the expense of powder and lead would be saved. About 100 years later Benjamin Franklin declared his support for bows and arrows, and 1784 saw the formation of the Archers division of the Honourable Artillery Company. Although the idea of making it a military body could hardly have been seriously contemplated, a manuscript book dated 1789, containing carefully executed drawings of archery implements, depicted a bow with a bayonet to screw onto the end of it, which was possibly the weapon that the division used. In 1794 the Court of Assistants passed a resolution 'that it be recommended to the Archers division to adopt some better mode of arming themselves, so as to become more efficient on their joining the battalion on public emergencies'.

During the latter years of the eighteenth century England had not only been involved in war and the threat of war with America and France, she had also faced the prospect

The last of the Bowmen

The Ladies Volunteers in full March to be imbodied under the Gentlemen Heroes in the different Camps at Coxheath War Command 1778. *So desperate was Parliament to find enough able-bodied men to fight the American war of 1775-83 that debtors, felons, boys and middle-aged men, and even Roman Catholics were impressed. Cornwallis's own 33rd, mustered at Coxheath in Kent shortly before embarkation in 1779 for the Siege of Charleston, included seventy-six women and forty-two children on its rolls. This contemporary cartoon provides a satirical view of the man-power shortage, plus a suggestive double-entendre in its caption*

of arming against Russia and the problems of protecting her own shores against invasion. Much of the time of the government had been taken up by negotiating settlements, planning defence measures and being criticized for any extravagance and every expenditure on military matters. Richard Oswald Mason had obviously thought seriously about the problems that were besetting his country. As a patriot he made his contribution in a seriously thought-out, although quite impractical, scheme for equipping pikemen with longbows. The publication of his book *Considerations for the Reasons that exist for Reviving the use of the Long Bow with the Pike etc.*, in 1798, added yet another considered plea for the re-adoption of archery to nearly three centuries of protest at its discontinuance. He used as his dedication *Pro Aris et Focis*—'for altar and home'.

Mason was the last advocate for the general use of the bow in war and he urged that, as it was intended to have a general arming of the people, and as possibly many of them, from necessity, would be armed only with pikes, it was advisable that they should also have bows. In his book Mason outlines 'The Manual Exercise of the Bow and the Pike', and one wonders with what emotion the members of the rank and file would have viewed these rather complicated manœuvres, and what their reactions would have been to being equipped with a bow, a quiver with twenty-four arrows, a broad sword, and a specially designed ten-foot pike with supports. A sample of the pike could be viewed at Mr. Thomas Waring's Manufactory, Charlotte Street, Bloomsbury, a well-known supplier of archery goods of the day.

The notes that Mason gives on the training of these archer-pikemen are cursory—'The use of the bow is so generally known ... that it is not necessary to be very particular.' He is, however, particular to point out that the quiver should be worn on the left, a most awkward arrangement, and that the bow should have a drawing power of sixty pounds or more. He goes on to suggest a rough and ready method of judging distances, and finally and rather ambitiously claims that daily practice for a month is sufficient to prepare a bowman for the line. From these and other details it is quite certain that Mason was a theorist on specialist warfare rather than properly versed in the art of archery.

209

But there was a practical use of the conventional form of bow in war in the nineteenth century, too. Archers of India were opponents to British forces at a comparatively late period. In the army defending Shah Najaf, during the second relief of Lucknow in 1857, there was a large body of archers on the walls, armed with composite bows and arrows which were used 'with great force and precision'.

A sergeant of the 93rd Highlanders raised his head above the wall and was lucky to survive an arrow which was shot completely through his bonnet. Not so lucky was another soldier, too curious for his own safety, as Sergeant-Major Mitchell reported: 'One poor fellow of the 93rd, named Penny, of No. 2 Company, raising his head for an instant a little above the wall, got an arrow right through the brain, the shaft projecting more than a foot out at the back of his head. . . .' In revenge the men gave a volley of fire, 'and one unfortunate man of the regiment, named Montgomery, of No. 6 Company, exposed himself a little too long to watch the effect of our volley, and before he could get down into shelter again an arrow was sent through his heart, passing clean through his body and falling on the ground a few yards behind him. He leaped about six feet straight up into the air and fell stone dead.' This rare report is a vivid testimony of the lethal power of an accurately aimed shaft. The effectiveness of such defence must have been limited to the total stocks of arrows available, in the same way that modern armies rely on a constant supply of ammunition for their survival. There is evidence of hastily assembled stocks of arrows of any sort or condition, as one private collection reveals. In it there are arrows with points roughly fashioned from nails, slivers of tin-cans, broken blades— in fact anything suitable which could be attached to an arrow-shaft—in marked contrast to the fine workmanship and design which is typical of good-quality Indian arrows made for war and the chase.

Until the reforms of 1905–06 the Chinese constitution provided for two sorts of military organization, the Manchu army and the Chinese armies of the provinces. The latter resembled a local constabulary rather than an army; its soldiers were poorly paid, virtually untrained and badly armed. The Manchu army was the hereditary national army, and every adult male was entitled by birth to be enrolled under one of the eight banners and to draw an

Crudely and hastily made arrows used in the Indian Mutiny of 1857, a desperate attempt to defy the British military power

allowance of rice, whether or not employed on active service. Both armies were equipped with the traditional composite bow up to at least 1900, when a report in *The Sphere* concludes: 'A great portion of the Chinese army is still armed with this type of bow.'

These were the troops who took part in the large-scale rebellions in the 1850s and the 1860s; it was these who fought against Japan in the 1894–95 war, and who were involved in the Boxer Rebellion of 1900. It was not until after the Russo-Japanese War of 1904–05 that attempts were made to reorganize the Chinese armies on European lines, and military schools and training organizations were set up in addition to the re-arming of the troops with more modern weapons. Previous to this the rank of 'Archery Inspector' in each unit was an important post, and it was he who was responsible for training bowmen in the old arts of archery in war. The traditions and customs of bow and arrow warfare, which had been introduced by the invading Mongols, had lasted without change and almost without challenge for 700 years, right into living memory.

In the examples of the use of the bow in various situations as part of modern warfare, it is not surprising to note that where this has occurred it has been among peoples who have historically used the bow as a major weapon. There are also a few instances where exponents in the art of shooting, or

211

those who have become fascinated by the potentialities of archery as a weapon of war, have promoted one-man campaigns to reintroduce the bow for specialized uses. Both of these aspects emerged during the Second World War of 1939–45.

In 1940, during the first summer after the outbreak of war, England frantically prepared to defend her shores against an expected invasion by German forces. In the event a belated attempt in the late autumn went off like a damp squib; but in the meanwhile Peter Fleming, the noted writer, found himself in charge of a small unit, part of a hurriedly mobilized defence force. He subsequently wrote of his experiences, and the following extract from *The Spectator* conveys the almost holiday-like atmosphere of those hot summer days of the 'phoney war'.

'Twelve Corps, who were responsible for the defence of Kent and half Sussex, held the sector most obviously threatened by invasion. The troops were thin on the ground and under-equipped and the Corps Commander (General 'Bulgey' Thorne) had to envisage at least the possibility that the Germans might establish a bridgehead which he would be unable to contain, and thus force him to withdraw to previously prepared positions (surely the most ominous words in the military vocabulary) behind the Stop-Line. Anything likely thereafter to delay or interfere with the enemy's preparations to assault the Stop-Line would clearly be of value; and I found myself charged with the duty of organizing some sort of guerrilla force which would allow itself to be overrun by the invaders and thereafter harass them to the best of its ability. . . .

'My own small force was based in a huge tract of woodland on top of a ridge, and we had not been there very long before I procured, at the taxpayers' expense, two large bows and a supply of arrows and told the Lovat Scouts to learn how to use them. This measure was perhaps not as silly as it sounds. . . . From this friendly jungle we reckoned we should be able to operate with much convenience at night, and we made a particular study of the approaches to various large country houses which stood on or near its outskirts and which were likely to be used as headquarters by German units or formations. By day, however, we expected that we should have to lie up, and the question then arose of

212

what action we should take against any enemy who entered the wood. Merely to lie low until they had gone away again would be bad for our morale and mean neglecting an opportunity of harassing the invader, which was what we were there for. On the other hand, to engage the enemy with our normal weapons would advertise our presence in the wood and might lead to the destruction of our base.

'This, in theory, is where the bows and arrows came in. For whatever purpose and in whatever strength the enemy entered the wood—whether we were dealing with a solitary botanist or a fighting patrol—we knew that he would move on the rides and tracks and we knew that some of him would get lost. If he presented a target at all, he would present it at very close range; and it was at least on the cards that circumstances would arise in which a silent arrow could advantageously be used when a noisy bullet could not.

'We realized, of course, that if we did implant an arrow in one of our would-be conquerors, the chances were against our implanting it in a vital spot and that he might get away and give the alarm; but we consoled ourselves with the belief that a casualty of so unexpected a nature would have a distracting effect upon the mind of the German High Command and that exaggerated versions of it would arouse awe and misgivings in their troops. Our purpose was to cause delay and diversion, and the diversionary effect on a modern army of wounding one of its soldiers with an arrow is probably less trivial than the effect of shooting half-a-dozen of them dead with more orthodox missiles.

'In the end the only living target ever engaged with our bows was a fallow deer, which I hit far back, following up for hours and finally lost. We did, however, find a real though limited use of bows and arrows on night operations. You strap a detonator and short length of safety-fuse to the arrow and, having reached the perimeter of the position you are attacking, you light the safety fuse and fire the arrow over the heads of the outposts, thus causing a brisk and unexplained explosion within their lines and often creating a certain amount of confusion.

'This was (as far as I know) the nearest the British soldier has come for several centuries to discharging an arrow in anger, and on the whole I think it is probably just as well that in 1940 he never had to come any nearer.'

As it happened, unknown to Fleming, in the May of 1940, a British soldier shot and killed a German on French soil with a well-aimed arrow.

Jack Churchill had been a member of the British team in the World Archery Championship at Oslo earlier in 1939, and before embarking for France he had made a powerful yew bow and some hunting arrows. He first used one of these while on patrol beyond the Maginot Line, the German positions being some sixty yards ahead. Frustrated and irritated by the official policy of not provoking the enemy, Captain Churchill decided upon a symbolic gesture which he thought would not only give him great personal satisfaction but might also create a certain alarm, despondency and bewilderment in the enemy lines. On 31 December, 1939, whilst out with a patrol amid the undulating, snow-covered countryside of no-man's-land, he stealthily made his way to between fifty and eighty yards from the German lines and, drawing his bow-string back to his cheek, let loose an arrow which he heard bite into the frost-hard ground with an audible 'clack'. There was no reaction whatsoever, so Churchill again drew his bow and loosed a second arrow. This time a German voice called out, and there was obviously some consternation caused in the enemy defences, although he did not have the satisfaction of knowing whether or not his arrow had hit anyone.

In the *War Diary* of the 4th Infantry Brigade the following paragraph appears: 'One of the reassuring sights of the embarkation was the sight of Captain Churchill passing down the beach with his bows and arrows! His actions in the Saar with his arrows are known to many and his disappointment at not having had the chance to keep in practice had tried him sorely.' However, the incident that won Jack Churchill fame, the result of eccentric enthusiasm, took place on 27 May, 1940, while he was in command of a mixed force holding the village of L'Epinette, near Béthune, during the retreat to Dunkirk.

Climbing into the loft of a small granary, through a vertical opening in one wall normally used for hauling up sacks of grain, Captain Churchill saw, some thirty yards away, five German soldiers sheltering behind the wall but in clear view of the granary. Quickly and quietly Churchill fetched up two infantrymen and instructed them to open rapid fire on the enemy but not to pull the trigger until he had loosed an arrow at the centre man. He lifted his bow, took careful aim and loosed the shaft. At the same time as the bow-string twanged, the air was shattered by the rapid fire of the two infantrymen. Captain Churchill was delighted to see his arrow strike the centre German in the left of the chest and penetrate his body; the remaining Germans of the party slumped to the ground. With the idea of retrieving his arrow by pushing it through the wound, Captain Churchill swiftly ran to the body but was unable to extract the shaft. In his haste he broke the arrow, leaving its barbed head in the German's body. At this moment enemy machine-gun fire was opened down the line of the road and everyone dived for cover.

Five years before the first atomic bomb exploded and nearly 600 years after the Battle of Crécy, an English archer had incongruously and briefly returned to the ancient battlefields of France.

This was a time during which every avenue was explored, no matter how unlikely, to discover special-purpose or 'secret' weapons, and some rather self-conscious attempts were made by the authorities to investigate the possibilities of using bows and arrows by special army units. A firm which had begun making a new design of tubular steel competition bows received an enquiry about the production of these bows for use by Commandos as a silent weapon. The United States army included bows and arrows among the weapons tested for possible use by cloak and dagger units, and the Australian army was also interested in the employment of archery by its troops; but none of these investigations seem to have been followed up. Another wartime enthusiast, Anders Lassen, V.C., distinguished himself in very successful raids upon the French coast and in the celebrated attack on the Island of Sark which resulted indirectly in the chaining of British prisoners of war. Lassen was a keen archer and wrote a letter to the War Office in the hope of arousing their interest in military training with bows and arrows. Under the heading *Bow and Arrow used in modern warfare*, he wrote:

'The thought may appear ridiculous, perhaps even stupid, to those who are not aware what a wonderful weapon it is.

'That we should continue to use in 1941 the same weapon

which won victory for the English in the Hundred Years War may seem impossible when one compares the bow with a machine-gun or a tommy-gun.

'However, after having attended different training schools and according to what I know about guerrilla warfare, scout patrols raiding-patrols and all that sort of thing, I have no doubt that bow and arrows would in many cases prove of great value.

'I have considerable experience in hunting with bow and arrow. I have shot everything from sparrows to stags, and although I have never attempted to shoot a man yet, it is my opinion that the result would turn out just as well as with stags.

Advantages:
1. The arrow is almost soundless.
2. The arrow kills without shock or pain, so is unlikely, shall we say, that a man would scream or do anything like that.
3. A well-trained archer can shoot up to fifteen shots a minute.
4. The arrow is as deadly as an ordinary bullet.
5. Actually one does not aim, which at night would be a great advantage—it is more like the way one throws a stone.

Disadvantages:
1. It is extremely difficult and demands a great deal of training and interest for the job.

'A good suitable bow made for the purpose would today cost in London from £2 to £6, practice arrows four shillings apiece and can be used several hundreds of times. Hunting arrows would be about twice as dear.'

A. F. E. V. S. Lassen

At this time Lassen and his group of Commandos were in training at Achnacarry, in the Highlands of Scotland, and shortly after writing his letter two bows with arrows arrived from the War Office. Whether or not this was due to his letter it is not known. However, the fact remains that the Dane was happy to be able to begin battle training somewhat incongruously equipped with bows and arrows. We do not know how or when Anders Lassen used these weapons in action; his biographer (his mother) is understandably silent on the subject, but it would be reasonable

216

to assume that he made full use of his deadly toys. The appearance of the bow in modern warfare was an anachronism, tolerated rather than openly encouraged by the fact that those who employed such eccentric means to kill the enemy were individually exceptional soldiers to be humoured and encouraged.

Perhaps the most dramatic accounts of the use of the bow and arrow in modern times are those from the victims themselves—at least from those who survived the indignity of being a live target. It is rare, these days, to find an individual unwittingly falling victim to a stray arrow, but William Kinsman, just a year or so ago, happily survived a colleague's wayward shaft at a meeting of fellow archers in London. The precise details of the incident are of little importance; what is of great interest to us is a first-hand account from Kinsman which describes his sensations at the moment of near fatality.

'The arrow struck before I was aware that I was to be a human target, at a distance of about 14 to 15 yards it hit the left side of my chest with tremendous impact, almost taking away my breath, it cut a neat hole in my shirt and travelled on into my chest. I am not sure how far it entered, but it was sufficient to puncture and deflate my lung. I felt little or no pain and, apart from the shock of the impact, I had no discomfort except for the blood which began to well up in my mouth. I was fortunate in that the shaft missed my heart by about three inches and that it was merely a target arrow which I removed quite easily. Had it been barbed or tanged the outcome could have been quite serious.' Mr. Kinsman had the facilities of modern medicine to help him; without such prompt aid there is little doubt that he would have quickly bled to death—a fate undoubtedly suffered by many victims of the bow and arrow in battle.

Apart from those areas of the world where the gun has not yet gained full superiority, archery in battle, used as a tactical weapon and as part of a grand overall design of war, has now been superseded by other, more deadly, but less romantic, weapons. In all probability the archers of Asia, the bowmen of Europe and the tribes scattered over most of the world, had little conception of the subtle technicalities that control missile projection. None the less, over the centuries countless millions of arrows have been discharged and have found their fatal marks with the help of a unique and persistent instinct which has subconsciously incorporated the more scientific aspects of ballistics, kinetic energy and mathematics. Without the bow, the battlefields of the world throughout many millennia would have been strangely primitive, and the dominance of many kings and commanders would have more easily crumbled or may have remained more stable. New forms of warfare would have had to have waited until the arrival of gunpowder, and matters of defence would not have evolved in the way they did.

There is little doubt that the bow remains the most influential weapon yet in actual warfare, a position that could now be challenged by modernists of the Atomic Age; but it is incontestably the most ancient and long-lived of any missile weapon invented by man.

"It's immune to jamming, undetectable by radar, creates no fall-out . . ."

Selected Reading

The following short list of books has been chosen as a basis for a more detailed background to the historical periods and specific events which have been dealt with in this history. The technical aspects of archery, which include various forms of bows and their construction, and both theoretical and practical studies of their performance, are subjects outside this bibliography. In this connection, the reader is directed to the important bibliography by Fred Lake and Hal Wright, *A Bibliography of Archery*, 1974.

Brown, Dee *Bury My Heart at Wounded Knee*, 1971
Burne, Alfred H. *The Crécy War*, 1955
Burne, Alfred H. *The Agincourt War*, 1956
Catlin, George *Letters and Notes on the Manners, Customs and Condition of the North American Indians*, 1841
Cowper, H. S. *The Art of Attack*, 1906
Creasy, Sir Edward *Fifteen Decisive Battles*, 1902
Custer, Gen. G. A. (edited) *My Life on the Plains*, 1963
Draeger, Donn F. and Smith, Robert W. *Asian Fighting Arts*, ND
Featherstone, Donald *The Bowmen of England*, 1967
Fenwick, Kenneth, (Ed.) *The Third Crusade*, 1958
Frere, Sheppard *Britannia*, 1967
Froissart, Sir John (Trs. Thomas Johnes) *Chronicles of England, France, Spain and the Adjoining Countries*, 1839
Green, Peter *Alexander the Great*, 1970
Grose, Francis *Military Antiquities respecting a history of the English Army*, 1786
Hamilton, T. M. *Native American Bows*, 1972
Hardy, Robert *Longbow*, 1976
Hearn, Ethel H. *The Sagas of Olaf Tryggvason and of Harold the Tyrant*, 1911
Heath, E. G. *The Grey Goose Wing*, 1971
Heath, E. G. (Ed.) *Bow versus Gun*, 1973
Heath, E. G. and Chiara, Vilma *Brazilian Indian Archery*, 1977
Herodotus (Trs. George Rawlinson) *History of the Greek and Persian Wars*, 1966
Hibbert, Christopher *Agincourt*, 1964
Keegan, John *The Face of Battle*, 1976
Keller, Werner *The Etruscans*, 1975
Latham, J. D. and Paterson, W. F. *Saracen Archery*, 1970
Latham, Ronald (Trs.) *The Travels of Marco Polo*, 1958
Lemmon, Lt.-Col. Charles H. *The Field of Hastings*, 1956
Livius, Titus (Trs. Aubrey de Sélincourt) *The War with Hannibal*, 1965
Lloyd, Alan *The Hundred Years War*, 1977
Machen, Arthur *The Bowmen and other Legends of the War*, 1915
McKee, Alexander *King Henry VIII's Mary Rose*, 1973
Mallett, Michael *Mercenaries and their Masters*, 1974
Mandel, Gabriele *The Life and Times of Genghis Khan*, 1970

Mason, Oswald *Use of the Long Bow with the Pike*, 1798

Montgomery of Alamein *A History of Warfare*, 1968

Morrissey, Frank R. *Samurai Archery*, 1960

Murdock, James *A History of Japan*, 1926

Neade, William *The Double-armed Man*, 1625

Nicolas, Sir Harris *History of the Battle of Agincourt*, 1832

Oman, Charles *A History of the Art of War*, 1898

Phillips, E. D. *The Royal Hordes; Nomad People of the Steppes*, 1965

Pope, Saxton T. *A Study of Bows and Arrows*, 1923

Powick, Sir Maurice *The Battle of Lewes 1264*, 1964

Rausing, Gad *The Bow, some notes on its origin and development*, 1967

Rickert, Edith (Comp.) *Chaucer's World*, 1948

Rowse, A. L. *Bosworth Field*, 1966

Seward, Desmond *The Hundred Years War*, 1978

Singh, Sarva Daman *Ancient Indian Warfare*, 1965

Smythe, John (Ed. John Hall) *Certain Discourses Military*, 1964

Stenton, Sir Frank (Ed.) *The Bayeux Tapestry*, 1957

Thucydides (Trs. Benjamin Jowett) *The Peloponnesian Wars*, 1966

Turnbull, S. R. *The Samurai, a military history*, 1977

Viollet-le-Duc, M. *Dictionnaire Raisonné de Mobilier Francais*, 1874

Walker, G. Goold *The Honourable Artillery Company*, 1926

Wallace, William J. *Hupa Warfare*, 1949

Warner, Philip *The Soldier*, 1975

Wise, Terence *1066, Year of Destiny*, 1979

Woolmer-Williams, Capt. *Incidents in the history of the Honourable Artillery Company*, 1888

Yadin, Yigael *The Art of Warfare in Biblical Lands*, 1963

Acknowledgements

The publishers have made every effort to contact the owners of all copyright material, and apologize for any omissions due to difficulties in tracing such sources. While the majority of the illustrations are from the author's own collection, permission has very kindly been granted to reproduce the following: page 16, Musée de Louvre; 17, Roger Wood; 19, the Metropolitan Museum of Art (photography by Egyptian Expedition); 30, American Numismatic Society; 46, 47, 48, Phaidon Press; 56, 62, Bibliothèque de la Bourgeoisie de Berne; 65, 168, 173, Trustees of the British Museum; 76, The Frick Collection, New York; 113, Christ Church Library, Oxford; 127, the Master and Fellows of Trinity College, Cambridge; 143, 147, Bibliothèque Nationale; 149, Photographie Giraudon; 175, Dr. Charles E. Grayson; 179, University of California; 198, Schultz-Guidon. We have been unable to trace sources for the illustrations on pages 73 and 218.

To develop particular aspects of this history, certain passages have been extracted from *The Grey Goose Wing* (Osprey 1971), now out of print. Reference has been made to articles in the *Journal* of the Society of Archer-Antiquaries too numerous to mention, which have been of special interest.

Index

Index